Cambridge Elements

Elements in Global Philosophy of Religion
edited by
Yujin Nagasawa
University of Oklahoma

ZOROASTRIANISM AND CONTEMPORARY PHILOSOPHY

Daniel Nolan
University of California, Santa Cruz

Shaftesbury Road, Cambridge CB2 8EA, United Kingdom

One Liberty Plaza, 20th Floor, New York, NY 10006, USA

477 Williamstown Road, Port Melbourne, VIC 3207, Australia

314–321, 3rd Floor, Plot 3, Splendor Forum, Jasola District Centre,
New Delhi – 110025, India

103 Penang Road, #05–06/07, Visioncrest Commercial, Singapore 238467

Cambridge University Press is part of Cambridge University Press & Assessment, a department of the University of Cambridge.

We share the University's mission to contribute to society through the pursuit of education, learning and research at the highest international levels of excellence.

www.cambridge.org
Information on this title: www.cambridge.org/9781009555722

DOI: 10.1017/9781009555739

© Daniel Nolan 2025

This publication is in copyright. Subject to statutory exception and to the provisions of relevant collective licensing agreements, with the exception of the Creative Commons version the link for which is provided below, no reproduction of any part may take place without the written permission of Cambridge University Press & Assessment.

An online version of this work is published at doi.org/10.1017/9781009555739 under a Creative Commons Open Access license CC-BY-NC 4.0 which permits re-use, distribution and reproduction in any medium for non-commercial purposes providing appropriate credit to the original work is given and any changes made are indicated. To view a copy of this license visit https://creativecommons.org/licenses/by-nc/4.0

When citing this work, please include a reference to the DOI 10.1017/9781009555739

First published 2025

A catalogue record for this publication is available from the British Library

ISBN 978-1-009-55572-2 Hardback
ISBN 978-1-009-55571-5 Paperback
ISSN 2976-5749 (online)
ISSN 2976-5730 (print)

Cambridge University Press & Assessment has no responsibility for the persistence or accuracy of URLs for external or third-party internet websites referred to in this publication and does not guarantee that any content on such websites is, or will remain, accurate or appropriate.

For EU product safety concerns, contact us at Calle de José Abascal, 56, 1°, 28003 Madrid, Spain, or email eugpsr@cambridge.org

Zoroastrianism and Contemporary Philosophy

Elements in Global Philosophy of Religion

DOI: 10.1017/9781009555739
First published online: July 2025

Daniel Nolan
University of California, Santa Cruz
Author for correspondence: Daniel Nolan, dnolan1@ucsc.edu

Abstract: Zoroastrianism is a religion with a long history, but it has been comparatively neglected by contemporary philosophers. This Element aims to bring aspects of its long intellectual history into conversation with contemporary Anglo-American philosophy. Section 1 provides an introduction to Zoroastrianism and its history, some of the important texts, and some contemporary philosophy engaged with Zoroastrian themes. Section 2 discusses distinctive contributions Zoroastrian thought can make to the problems of evil and suffering. And, Section 3 discusses a 'quasi-universalist' approach to puzzles about heaven and salvation, inspired by Zoroastrian theological texts. This title is also available as Open Access on Cambridge Core.

Keywords: Zoroastrianism, philosophy of religion, problem of evil, problem of hell, universalism

© Daniel Nolan 2025

ISBNs: 9781009555722 (HB), 9781009555715 (PB), 9781009555739 (OC)
ISSNs: 2976-5749 (online), 2976-5730 (print)

Contents

1 Introduction to Zoroastrianism   1

2 Zoroastrianism and the Problems of Evil and Suffering   18

3 Zoroastrianism and Puzzles about Eternal Reward   36

References   60

1 Introduction to Zoroastrianism

Zoroastrianism is an immensely old religion, that has shaped and been shaped by many of the major world religions, while keeping a distinctive identity of its own. Along with religious practices and commitments, Zoroastrianism has also carried with it a distinctive body of thought, including thought that addresses questions about the fundamental nature and purpose of the world around us; about good and evil and living a good life; and about questions in the philosophy of religion, like the nature of the divine and what makes sense of suffering in this life.

I am not a Zoroastrian, nor am I a historian or theologian. My discipline is philosophy, and my aim in this Element is to exhibit some of the material in the Zoroastrian tradition that will be of interest to philosophers, particularly those working in the contemporary 'Anglo-American' tradition. My hope is that this will facilitate a fruitful exchange, and in particular that more people with backgrounds in contemporary philosophy will come to appreciate the riches of the Zoroastrian tradition and how it can provide useful theoretical alternatives and arguments when addressing questions of continuing philosophical interest. As should go without saying, this is not the only reason someone might be interested in the Zoroastrian intellectual tradition, and the value of that tradition in no way stands or falls with how interesting it might be to people outside that tradition. As I will repeatedly try to make clear in the discussions to follow, I do not claim to speak for Zoroastrianism or any of the many intellectual traditions that have flourished in the Zoroastrian community over the millennia.

There has been a growing movement in the past few decades to bring work on a wide range of philosophical traditions into English-speaking philosophy departments, and no doubt into philosophy departments where the languages of instruction and research writing are other European languages. One important strand of this movement has been a movement to represent 'Asian Philosophy'. I welcome better representation of work on a wide range of Asian philosophical traditions, as well as work in other traditionally underrepresented traditions, but to date, much of the work on Asian philosophy has focused on a few strands of the rich philosophical heritage of Asia. Philosophical writings in some Buddhist schools have received significant amounts of attention, and significant attention has been paid to the traditional six *āstika* schools of Vedic Indian philosophy, and to some work in the Confucian and Daoist traditions.

This does not exhaust the traditions being brought into dialogue with contemporary philosophical work, nor being studied without an eye to contemporary connections in English-speaking philosophy departments. But I think it is fair to say that attention has still been lop-sided, with some philosophical traditions still largely neglected. Perhaps this is inevitable: I am not sure what 'working equally on every philosophical tradition' could even mean in practice, especially since philosophical traditions can be subdivided into further traditions. Still, it would be better if there was more work bringing a wider range of traditions of philosophical thought into engagement with contemporary philosophical discussions. (Better for contemporary discussions, at least!) One of the motives I have in writing this Element is to promote more useful engagement with Zoroastrian philosophical thought by academics working in philosophy departments. Though more engagement with Zoroastrian philosophical thought outside the academy is welcome as well!

This Element is, in some ways, a work of comparative philosophy. This is not the only way to approach philosophical material and themes in Zoroastrian works. Another obvious one would be to encounter this material on its own terms from within a Zoroastrian intellectual tradition. I am not the person to attempt a work on Zoroastrian philosophy in that style, but I would read it with interest. I have taken one approach that I hope will be illuminating and draws on my own expertise. For those who find this approach limited or idiosyncratic, I would encourage them to bring Zoroastrian philosophical thought to audiences in their own way.

There are many interesting philosophical issues addressed by Zoroastrian literature that I will not be covering in this Element, partly for reasons of space and partly because there is no doubt much of philosophical interest that I have not digested yet. In Section 1.4.2, I mention some other contemporary engagement with philosophical themes in Zoroastrianism, though there is much more material to be engaged with. In particular, ethics and questions of how to live have been an important concern of Zoroastrian writers, and a central tenet of Zoroastrianism is that an adherent should practice 'good thoughts, good words, and good deeds'. I anticipate that distinctively Zoroastrian takes on questions of what to aim for, what to do, and what sort of person to be can be fruitfully brought into dialogue with contemporary work on ethics by philosophers, but there is not space in this Element to contribute to this task here.

If this Element is successful, it will spark much more engagement with the Zoroastrian tradition by those interested in contemporary philosophical debates. I hope this and subsequent work will be of interest to those with Zoroastrian backgrounds, but also to those who are interested in learning from intellectual perspectives that have been comparatively ignored by contemporary academic philosophy.

1.1 Structure of the Element

This is an Element of three sections, and you are reading the first. The rest of this section will contain several kinds of introductory material: a brief history of Zoroastrianism; a discussion of the main Zoroastrian texts I will be engaging with; and a section on further readings about Zoroastrian intellectual history and some other philosophical discussions of Zoroastrianism in the literature that I will not have room to adequately cover here. The goal of this section is not just to situate this Element, but to give readers who may have no previous familiarity an orientation that will hopefully help get them started in engaging with the philosophical themes in Zoroastrian thought, should they wish to do that further.

Section 2 will discuss the problems of evil and suffering as they arise in a Zoroastrian framework. The cosmos is ruled by an incredibly powerful and incredibly benevolent being, the great god Ahura Mazda, according to the overwhelming majority of Zoroastrian traditions. Yet we encounter disorder, evil and suffering all around us. (I hope you, dear reader, are not currently dealing with much evil and suffering. But turning on the news is enough to remind us that there is a lot of both in the world.) Zoroastrianism, like for example, the Abrahamic religions, faces the challenge of explaining why this evil and suffering has not been eliminated by the deity. I will focus on two lines of response at least arguably found in the Zoroastrian tradition, though these are not the only responses reflected in Zoroastrian writing. According to the first, it is a lack of omnipotence that explains why Ahura Mazda has not yet triumphed over evil. According to this option, the struggle with Angra Mainyu is a real contest, and not even Ahura Mazda can secure an immediate and total victory over evil and suffering. The second potential response is that even an omnipotent deity would allow evil and suffering in order that those who struggle against it can gain merit by doing so. In turn, this means their eventual reward will be even more valuable: not only will they have an eternal and blissful afterlife, it will be *even better* to the extent that it is merited. Both of these responses to the problem of evil and suffering face potential objections, and some of the more pressing objections to them will also be discussed.

Lastly, Section 3 engages with a related issue that arises not just for Zoroastrianism but for many religious traditions. Zoroastrianism postulates an afterlife, which involves at least two stages. There is some kind of existence of people in a spiritual form in the years after death. But one day, the Zoroastrian tradition says, the whole material world will be transformed by the final triumph of good over evil. In the final stages of that process, everyone who had died will be bodily resurrected, and everyone will be present for the final elimination of evil in the world. Those who remain after that final cleansing will have an eternal, blissful, and embodied life. There are some philosophical puzzles about stories of blissful afterlives, whether material or immaterial. These often concern the question of how an omnibenevolent deity should organise such an afterlife. Should such a being grant everyone eternal bliss? If not, how can the division be made between 'the sheep and the goats': how could it be fair or just to grant one person infinite bliss but deny it to someone else almost as worthy of that reward? The Zoroastrian tradition, I will argue, can offer some distinctive answers to the philosophical puzzles about eternal rewards, and in particular suggests a kind of 'quasi-universalism', where everyone participates in the infinite reward of a future life, but to varying degrees.

No doubt, Zoroastrians take up a wide range of attitudes to the religion they belong to, including rejecting the 'Zoroastrian' presuppositions Sections 2 and 3 begin with. I have no argument even with, for instance, a Zoroastrian who performs the expected rituals but does not let their faith affiliation affect their theological or philosophical beliefs at all. I will be making many claims about what can be found in the Zoroastrian tradition, and from time to time will cite works that many Zoroastrians think have some authority, or at least are worthy of respect. But exploring options from starting points in Zoroastrian thought is not saying what all Zoroastrians do or should think, any more than engaging with a thinker in the Christian tradition yields doctrines that every Christian should adopt, or engaging with someone writing in a Buddhist tradition yields conclusions that all Buddhists must endorse. For readers interested in some of the range of views contemporary Parsi Zoroastrians have to questions of religion, practice, and morals, Kreyenbroake and Munshi 2001 contain a wealth of interviews of Parsis living in India, though of course the full range of diversity of opinions of self-identified Zoroastrians will go much further than even Kreyenbroake and Munshi captured.

1.2 A Brief Historical Sketch

Zoroastrianism begins with a prophet. He is often called 'Zoroaster' in English, following the name he was known by to the Greeks and Romans, but his name in his native language is better approximated by 'Zarathustra'. His family name is 'Spitama', and he appears to be descended from a line of priests. The reports of his revelations from Ahura Mazda, plus a core of sacred hymns traditionally attributed to him as their composer, form the core of the most sacred texts of Zoroastrianism. (The text concerning his message from Ahura Mazda is known as the *Gathas*, and the seven hymns in a similar language are known as the *Yasna Haptanhaiti*.) There is little consensus about where and when he lived. The orthodoxy among Western scholars seems to be coalescing around the view that he lived somewhere between 1600 BCE and 800 BCE, and likely in the northeastern lands of the Iranian peoples, perhaps in or near modern Uzbekistan. (In this paragraph and what follows, I have not followed the practice of representing names with non-English symbols. While, for example, it would be more faithful to the original texts to write Zarathustra's name as *staraϑuštra-* or *zarduxšt*, depending on the source, it does hurt readability for those not familiar with the scholarly transliteration schemes.)

The central part of Zarathustra's message is that there is a great struggle afoot between the good deity Ahura Mazda (in later languages often called Ohrmazd, Ormazd, or Hormizd) and his opponents, headed by the wrathful and evil spirit Angra Mainyu (later Ahriman). Each has a host of assistants and followers. Chief among Ahura Mazda's are the Amesha Spentas, or Holy Immortals, who may be associated with aspects of Ahura Mazda himself, since they have names that translate, for instance, as 'Good Purpose' or 'Immortality'. There are other divine beings on Ahura Mazda's side as well: from the earliest texts these include Mithra, a divine being associated with fire and justice, and later in the Zoroastrian tradition beings such as Anahita, the divine 'lady of the waters', assume prominence.

Angra Mainyu stands at the head stands at the head of a host of daiwas, devils, or supernatural evil creatures. The world is the venue of the great struggle between good and evil, and Zoroastrians are called to play a role in this struggle, primarily through rituals and good deeds. Zarathustra contrasts the actions of the good people with the 'followers of the lie', who serve Angra Mainyu's purposes, and may indeed worship daiwas.

Zarathustra's teachings came with a lot of ritual instruction, especially chants and hymns to recite, to ritual instructions such as the appropriate treatment of fire, the earth, and requirements of personal purity. Many of the rituals are the domain of a priestly class. The performance of rituals and other good deeds assist the forces of good in the great struggle, which will one day resolve in the victory of Ahura Mazda over Angra Mainyu. The faithful will be rewarded with a post-death sacred existence, interpreted by the later tradition as being full of joy and good things: an early account of heaven or paradise. Zoroastrians, both priests and laypeople, contribute to the great struggle against evil, and will share in the great reward brought by the eventual victory against the forces of darkness.

While I have attempted to stay close to standard Zoroastrian understandings of Zarathustra's message, it is not uncontroversial among scholars that there is this sort of ethical message in Zarathustra's teachings. See, for example, Cantera 2015 for a discussion of the views of revisionary scholars, especially those who see little or no ethical dimension in Zarathustra's teaching, and see the promise of a desirable afterlife as the reward for the highest levels of ritual rather than any moral behaviour. It is also controversial whether Zarathustra was even a real historical figure: see Hintze 2013 for a critical discussion of Zarathustra's historical reality. Whatever Zarathustra's intentions, the tradition he began eventually put at its centre notions of good and evil and the importance of choice between them. For an attempt to sum up the overall message of Zarathustra's works, see Boyce 1997.

The spread of Zoroastrianism in the centuries after Zarathustra's death is hard to trace. His doctrines appear to have spread to a number of Iranian peoples, especially the Medes and the Persians, and a priestly class the Greeks called *magi* were well established by the time the Greeks started recording information about the Medes and Persians. To judge from images, as well as eventual written records, the priestly class seems to have been in charge of the most sacred Zoroastrian rituals. The priesthood appears to have eventually been hereditary: not all sons of a priest were automatically priests, but coming from a priestly lineage was a necessary condition for priesthood. The rituals and other sacred 'texts' of Zoroastrianism must have been transmitted orally, and the later importance of pronouncing key rituals word-for-word and even with the correct pronunciation is probably responsible for the accurate transmission of at least the central works like the Gathas and Yasnas. A central part of Zoroastrian communal worship involved sacred fires, and the most distinctive architecture of Zoroastrian religious foundations is the 'fire temple', where a fire is kept burning in a state of ritual purity, and is the focus of important rituals.

The priestly class of Zoroastrianism, which may have originally been the group known as *magi*, re-emerged with several classes of priests with different roles. Of central importance is the *mobed*, the central celebrant for some of the most important rituals. (These are also called mowbeds or mobads in some texts.) Another important role is the *herbad (/ervad)*, who does not have the same range of ritual authority but often assists a *mobed*. In the twentieth century, other kinds of clergy were developed, such as *mobedyars*, *paramobeds*, and *pasbans*. Most Zoroastrian groups still restrict priestly offices to men. From time to time various priestly officials have held various titles that raise them above the ordinary run of *mobeds*, at least in restricted geographical regions. The Sassanid kings appear to have appointed a 'mobed of mobeds' (*mobadan mobad*) to be a high priest, perhaps with enforcement powers over other mobeds in the kingdom. Since the sixteenth century the Parsis have had a position of *dastur,* which signifies a certain kind of religious authority, though Zoroastrianism appears to have a more decentralised structure of spiritual authority among mobeds than the complex hierarchies of some versions of Christianity, for example.

The first dateable traces of Zoroastrianism, or more strictly Mazdaism, in the written record date from the eighth century BCE. Surviving Assyrian and Elamite tablets from that period record Western Iranians, probably Medes, with names reconstructed as Mazdakk(u) and Mazdaka 'of Mazda', and a possible mention of Ahura Mazda himself in an Assyrian list of gods from the eighth or seventh century BCE (Boyce 1982, p. 15). So it is possible that Zoroastrianism was the faith of even the Western Iranian peoples as early as the eighth century BCE, though Boyce 1982, pp. 14–15 suggests that worship of Ahura Mazda, among other gods, may have been prevalent before conversion of the Western Iranians to Zoroastrianism.

Zoroastrianism bursts onto the historical scene with the rise of the Persian Achaemenid dynasty, particularly with the rise of Cyrus the Great (c600–c530 BCE). Cyrus overthrew his overlords the Medes before conquering a vast empire, and his successors ruled a vast empire until 330 BCE. Cyrus appears to have been a Zoroastrian, though he was also famed for his religious tolerance, and his Achaemenid successors all appear to have supported Zoroastrianism, with a wide-ranging program of construction of fire temples, financial and political support for mobeds, and a tendency from very early to treat Zoroastrianism as the primary religion of the state, or at least of the Persians and the court. See Boyce 1982 for a comprehensive account of Zoroastrianism under the Achaemenids.

Famously, the Achaemenid empire was destroyed by the Macedonian Alexander the Great in his campaigns from 334 BCE to 324 BCE. The lands of that empire fell under the control of culturally Greek rulers of successor states, and many of the richest and most populated regions of their empire remained under the control of the 'successors' of Alexander until they were absorbed by Rome. However around 240 BCE, at the Eastern ends of the lands that were formerly controlled by the Achaemenids, an Iranian people called the Parthians overthrew their local Seleucid (Greek) overlords and established an empire of their own. The Parthians, so far as we can tell, were largely Zoroastrian, and their empire grew over the succeeding centuries until it was a peer competitor with the Roman Empire.

The Parthians eventually succumbed to a new Iranian empire, ruled by the Persian Sassanid dynasty. The Sassanids began as subject kings of the Parthians in Persia, but after defeating the Parthians in 224 CE, they moved to take over many of the lands previously ruled by the Parthian King and added to their domain territories in the East and North. The Sassanid royal house seems to have revived Achaemenid religious practices, and promoted themselves as protectors of the Zoroastrian faith, though they did not insist that their subjects in general embrace Zoroastrianism.

It was under the Sassanids that many important texts of Zoroastrianism were codified, including the two most important: the *Avesta* and the *Zand*. The Avesta is the central holy book of Zoroastrianism, and at its core are ritual texts and hymns in an especially ancient language that may be compositions of Zarathustra himself. The Zand is a set of translations and commentaries on the Avesta, many composed much later than the Avesta itself. Some surviving manuscripts present parts of the Zand interwoven with the Avestan texts they concern. See Section 1.3 for more discussion.

The Sassanid court appears to have attempted to impose an orthodoxy on the Zoroastrian faith. Some particularly informative inscriptions from around 290 CE describe the achievements of Kartir, one of the most powerful mobeds under a series of Sassanid kings. Kartir lists many accomplishments, including spreading rituals and temples of Zoroastrianism, converting people, and a 'striking down' of followers of a range of rival faiths, including Christians, Buddhists, Hindus, and Jews. He also boasts of the destruction of heretics and devil-worshippers. The impression given by this inscription is that some Sassanid monarchs attempted to impose an orthodoxy on Zoroastrianism as well as improve its position vis-a-vis other faiths in the multi-ethnic Zoroastrian empire. (For a useful summary of Kartir and his inscription, see Skjærvø 2012.)

With an attempt to impose orthodoxy came heterodox movements. I will briefly mention two heterodox traditions and one disputably orthodox one. The prophet Mani came to prominence in the Sassanid court, though he perhaps had a Gnostic Christian background. Mani preached a dualism according to which the spiritual world of divine light was ruled by the Father of Greatness, while the material world of darkness was ruled by the King of Darkness. We embodied beings are in the thrall of the evil spirit, and must seek release through ethical and ritual practices. Those of us who do not do enough to escape our material constraints in this world are bound to reincarnate until we eventually achieve release into a spiritual paradise of light. Mani's teachings founded a world religion, Manicheanism, that at its height spread East to India and China, and West to at least Carthage in North Africa, but perhaps throughout the Roman Empire. Since Mani's writings survive, and were formulated in a partly Zoroastrian intellectual background, they may shed some light on Zoroastrian thought of their time. But it is important to recognise that despite some similarities, Manicheanism has some important differences from Zoroastrianism. Zoroastrianism does not condemn the material world as an evil prison, and while there is a Zoroastrian emphasis on purity it is not in the cause of escaping the material world. This manifests in important social ways as well: the 'perfect' or the 'elect' in Manicheanism, those in the best place to escape our material prison, were supposed to not have children, in order not to re-trap more souls in this world. Zoroastrianism, on the other hand, has always valorised having children, especially by the mobed or priestly class.

The second tradition I want to briefly mention here is Mazdakism, named after the reformer Mazdak, who flourished in the sixth century CE. According to mainly hostile sources, Mazdak preached that property should be shared out evenly among believers, and even preached that women should be held in common. (Some interpreters think that instead he may have preached that powerful men should not have multiple women as wives or concubines while others had none.) Mazdakianism became a divisive doctrine, with rival factions in a disputed succession being identified as pro-Mazdak or anti-Mazdak, and Mazdak himself was executed when the anti-Mazdakian candidate secured power. There appears to have been a Mazdakian movement that long outlasted the death of its founder. Mazdakism is usually considered a variety of Zoroastrianism, perhaps an unorthodox one, rather than a rival religion like Manicheanism, and is an example of how Zoroastrian beliefs could vary widely, even under the Sassanids.

The third tradition I want to mention here is Zurvanism. (See Shaked 1992 and de Jong 2014, though de Jong takes a more deflationary approach to Zurvanism than I am inclined to.) At some point between the Achaemenid period and the reign of the Sassanid Shapur I, a tradition arose that Ahura Mazda and Angra Mainyu were brothers, the former good and the latter evil, and that they had a father, Zurvan, associated with time or infinite time. According to Zurvanism it was Zurvan who set the rules for the struggle between Ahura Mazda and Angra Mainyu, and while he is on Ahura Mazda's side, and can be prayed to, it is unclear whether he plays any active role after his initial setting events in motion.

Zurvanism seems to have been the dominant form of Zoroastrianism at the courts of some of the Sassanid kings, though it seems to have gone into decline once the Sassanids were overthrown by Muslim invaders. Perhaps it suffered in prestige because of its close association with the Sassanid court, or perhaps sophisticated conceptions of Zoroastrian doctrine were replaced by versions that survived in rural areas and regional centres, which perhaps were less touched in the first place by the fashion for Zurvanism.

The flourishing of Zoroastrianism under the Sassanids suffered a dramatic reversal between 642 CE and 651 CE, when the armies of Islam quickly overran the heart of the Sassanid empire. Conversion of the population to Islam was not quite as rapid: even after a period of rebellions and pacification, the former territory of the Sassanian state did not even become majority Muslim until well over a century after the conquest, and a Zoroastrian population continued in Iranian lands until today. Zoroastrians were not the only religious minority group in the former Sassanid empire under Islam: significant populations of Christians, Jews, and even Buddhists remained.

One significant development in the Zoroastrian community that occurred in the centuries after the Islamic conquest is that a group of Zoroastrians migrated to what is now India. The first group of Zoroastrians who made their home in India, especially in Gujarat, became known as the Parsis (i.e. people from Persia, or Pars/Fars). Some later groups who migrated to India became known as Iranis (i.e. people from Iran), though 'Parsi' is also used as an umbrella term for both of these communities, and I will be using it in this broader sense. 'Parsi' is also sometimes used for the ethnic group in India rather than for a religious affiliation. Sometimes in this work I will refer to Parsi doctrines in Zoroastrianism, but strictly speaking that is shorthand for talking about doctrines of Parsi Zoroastrianism.

The final major set of impacts on Zoroastrianism was a result of European colonialism. Important members of the Parsi community in Bombay and other cities became influential merchants, traders, and provided an interface between the markets of India, on the one hand, and European merchants such as those of the French, Dutch and British East India Companies on the other. One result of European penetration of Indian and Persian lands is that important diaspora communities of Zoroastrians have developed all over the world. While there are approximately 50,000 Zoroastrians in India, 15,000 in Iran, and significant though smaller populations in other traditional Zoroastrian homelands like the lands of modern-day Iraq, Uzbekistan, Tajikistan, and Pakistan, some of the largest national populations of Zoroastrians are found much further afield. The Zoroastrian population in the United States is approximately 15,000, with another 7,000 in Canada, and 4,000 in the United Kingdom. Even Australia has approximately 2,700 Zoroastrians, similar to the number in Tajikistan, where Zoroastrians have lived for thousands of years.

Another important impact on Zoroastrianism from the age of colonisation was downstream of first-hand contact between Western scholars and Zoroastrian texts, and later between Western scholars and Zoroastrian communities. Zoroastrianism and its texts became an object of academic study in the West, especially since Zoroastrianism appears to have influenced Judaism and eventually Christianity. Conclusions of early scholars in Europe have not always survived critical scrutiny, so readers should exercise caution reading older works making claims about what Zoroastrian doctrine is, or was in various historical periods. Particularly in India, Zoroastrians felt the need to articulate and define their doctrines in light of European interest and particularly in light of intellectual attacks on Zoroastrianism. Some Christian missionaries published a number of criticisms of Zoroastrian doctrine as part of an attempt to convert Parsis to Christianity, and various Zoroastrian authors wrote replies, not just addressing the arguments offered by critics but also informing Zoroastrians, particularly the laity, of what Zoroastrian doctrine really was (as they saw it). Maeck 1997 is a fascinating discussion of this development in Zoroastrian thought.

Many Zoroastrians have an understanding of their own faith and its history informed by the work of scholars of the nineteenth and twentieth centuries. Academic study of Zoroastrian topics is often pursued by non-Zoroastrians, and few of the most prominent scholars of Zoroastrianism have belonged to the faith. Part of the story here is presumably that resources for academic research are disproportionately concentrated in Europe, North America and other first-world regions, where Zoroastrian numbers are very low. There is some work being done on Zoroastrian thought in Iran, though my impression is that the priorities of the Islamic Republic are more focused on Muslim thought. In India, the K.R. Cama Oriental Institute in Mumbai is the premier centre of Zoroastrian learning, and it maintains a vital library of manuscripts as well as a series of active research and dissemination programs. While it may be a tribute to the intrinsic interest of the Zoroastrian tradition that it attracts attention well beyond the bounds of the Zoroastrian faith, it does mean that it is easier to get a view of how Zoroastrian thought is seen from the outside than its role in the living faith community.

Zoroastrianism today is practiced by one to two hundred thousand people worldwide, and it faces a wide range of challenges. It is a minority religion everywhere it is practiced, and it suffers persecution in some areas. Zoroastrians were one of the minority groups targeted by ISIS in Iraq, and some Zoroastrian asylum seekers from Iran claim that the religion has faced persecution there as well, though the Iranian government's official position is that it is a recognized and protected religious minority. In the diaspora, two of the main challenges many Zoroastrian groups face are younger generations not following the faith of their parents, and Zoroastrians marrying out of their communities. Many Zoroastrian groups in the diaspora maintain that for someone to become Zoroastrian, they must either have both parents of Zoroastrian ancestry, or at least that their father be of Zoroastrian ancestry. Even the more lenient of these two rules results in some mixed-faith marriages where the children are ineligible to become Zoroastrian, and in not allowing conversion of spouses who themselves lack the required ancestry, these rules have some tendency for those in mixed marriages to leave the Zoroastrian faith.

Zoroastrian communities both in the diaspora and in Iran and India are divided on whether conversions by people without Zoroastrian ancestry are to be allowed. Anita 2015 is an impassioned defence of the possibility of conversion, though he does maintain conversion should not be 'indiscriminate' (p xxviii). It remains to be seen what different Zoroastrian communities decide to do about the risk of a continuing decline in their numbers.

1.3 Important Texts

Zoroastrianism has a unique relationship to the central texts associated with it. The central holy book of Zoroastrianism is the *Avesta*, a compilation of texts put together sometime in the third to sixth centuries of the common era, somewhere in the Sassanid empire. Unfortunately, most of the Avesta has not survived, leaving the Zoroastrian faithful to rely on the parts that have survived, along with what can be gleaned from secondary discussions of the Avesta that appear to rely on parts that have not reached us. The Avesta itself seems to be a collection of texts composed in different periods. The latest parts of the Avesta, the so-called Young Avesta, are written in *Avestan*, a language that primarily survives in the Avesta texts themselves and some writings patterned after it. But some parts of the Avesta seem to be much older. The oldest parts are written in *Old Avestan* or *Gathic*. There are two parts to the very oldest texts. One is the Gathas, in the form of revelations from the prophet Zarathustra, often through reports of questions Zarathustra puts to Ahura Mazda and the replies he receives. The other is some of the hymns contained in the work. The Yasna Haptanhaiti, or seven great hymns of praise to various divine beings, seems to date from roughly the same period as the Gathas. It is believed that the Gathas is the composition of Zarathustra himself and that the seven great hymns are roughly contemporary with the Gathas. (Narten 1986 has argued that these early hymns are also the compositions of Zarathustra. See Hintze 2004 for a discussion of these seven important hymns.) Kanga 1997 is a recent translation of the Gathas into English.

These older works must have been transmitted verbally for a long time before they were written down, since the Iranian peoples only developed writing systems for any of their languages in Achaemenid times. (See Section 1.2 for speculation about when Zarathustra lived, for an estimate also of when the Gathas was composed.) The Avesta as a whole appears to have been compiled in Sassanid times. According to the Denkard, (to be discussed soon), it was arranged into twenty-one books or nasks, though some scholars have speculated that even this might not be correct, or it might get to twenty-one only by counting repeated material. Of the twenty-one books described, only one appears to have been transmitted in its entirety. A number have been transmitted partially, and some of the Avesta has been transmitted in fragmentary form, though exactly which texts were considered part of the Avesta is a continuing source of controversy.

Next, after the Avesta is the *Zand* or translations and explanations of the Avesta itself. This seems to have been compiled in the later Sassanid era. As well as providing important material in their own right, some seem to quote or reference parts of the *Avesta* that have not survived, and enable scholars to reconstruct the information in those sacred writings. Darmesteter (1880, 1893, 1897) remains an influential translation of the Avesta with the Zand, though obviously in need of some updating in light of the century-plus of scholarship since.

Beyond the Avesta and the Zand, there is a wide variety of texts, in a variety of languages, written by Zoroastrians and which are taken seriously as sources of religious and cultural information by at least some Zoroastrians. Instead of trying to list every Zoroastrian text of potential philosophical significance, I will restrict myself to describing some of the texts that are important for the purposes of this Element.

Several important texts seem to have been composed in the early Islamic period, perhaps as part of trying to articulate and preserve parts of the faith in the face of competition from Muslim scholars and clergy.

The *Denkard*, traditionally translated 'acts of the religion' though perhaps 'collection of wisdom' is a better translation, is an encyclopaedic work that appears to be an attempt to put in one place the teachings of Zoroastrianism, as they were known to the compiler. Some chapters have not survived, but after the Avesta and Zand the remaining chapters of the Denkard are probably the most comprehensive work representing a Zoroastrian understanding of the world surviving from this period. Gignoux 1994 is a good place to start in understanding its significance. Sanjana 1876 is the only complete translation into English of the surviving portions of the Denkard.

A less central work composed around the compiling of the Denkard is the *Škand Gumānīg Wizār* or the *Doubt Removing Book of Mardanfarrox* (Mardānfarrox 2015). It is primarily a work of apologetics, offering arguments in favour of Zoroastrianism and against rival religious traditions. This makes it particularly valuable to those seeking to understand Zoroastrian philosophy of religion in the period around when it was written. See Cereti 2014 for a discussion of its significance.

Another important work from a similar period is the *Bundahishn*, especially the so-called *Iranian Bundahishn*. The *Bundahishn* is a work in Middle Persian, perhaps mostly compiled in the late ninth century CE, with a focus on cosmological matters. (There are two main lines of manuscript survival, a shorter 'Indian Bundahishn' and a more comprehensive 'Iranian Bundahishn' or

'Greater Bundahishn', which appears to contain more of the original compilation.) It may be that parts of the Bundahishn are significantly older, and parts likely draw on material in now-lost sections of the *Avesta*. It is an important source for Zoroastrian myths about creation and the final fate of the world. Agostini and Thrope 2020 is the standard English translation of the Greater/Iranian Bundahishn, and I will be using their numbering of verses. Anklesaria 1956 remains another useful English translation.

The *Dadestan i Menog i-Khrad*, or the Judgements of the Spirits of Wisdom, sometimes referred to just as the *Menog i-Khrad* or the *Menog i-Xrad*, is in the form of a dialogue with the Spirit of Wisdom. As well as practical, moral, and ritual advice, it also contains an account of what will happen upon death and upon the final defeat of evil. It is possibly even earlier than the Denkard and Bundahishn in date, though dating it is a challenge. West 1885 still contains the standard translation.

The *Dadestan i Denig* is a book of questions and answers about the Zoroastrian religion, likely composed in the ninth century CE. Attached to some manuscripts of this work is a further set of discussions of controversial Zoroastrian questions. This additional text is known to scholars as the *Pahlavi Rivayat Accompanying the Dadestan i Denig*, and was perhaps composed in the tenth century CE. It contains several accounts of the Zoroastrian final judgement that will be relevant to Section 3 of this work. Williams 1983 is a valuable translation and textual discussion of this Rivayat.

Ulema i' Islam (also *Olma-i Islam*) is a text written in Iran in the aftermath of the Muslim invasion, perhaps in the tenth century CE. While its name means something like 'the learned of Islam', the setting of the text is a Zoroastrian mobed explaining to Islamic inquirers various things about the Zoroastrian faith. It exists in two forms (I and II), with important differences between them. Notably, one of them appears to endorse Zurvanism, which is otherwise much better known from foreigner's reports of Iranian religion than surviving Zoroastrian texts themselves. It contains material about a wide variety of Zoroastrian topics, often providing a different point of view from the Denkard and Bundahishn. A translation of it can be found in Dhabhar 1932.

Finally, the *Persian Rivayats* are an influential set of letters sent to the Parsi community in India from Zoroastrian experts in Iran in the fifteenth to eighteenth centuries. These have been more directly influential on Parsi communities than, for example, the Zoroastrians of Iran, but they contain valuable articulations of doctrines that it is difficult to locate elsewhere. The letters are responses to questions about Zoroastrian matters originating from the Parsi community and preserve in writing a lot of doctrine that would otherwise have been lost. Many of the most important of these letters are translated in Dhabhar 1932.

1.4 Secondary Literature, and the Current Literature on Zoroastrianism and Contemporary Philosophy

1.4.1 Guides to Zoroastrian Intellectual History

Two of the most valuable resources for reading more about Zoroastrianism are online and free. One is the comprehensive and peer-reviewed *Encyclopedia Iranica* (www.iranicaonline.org), covering not just Zoroastrian topics but a very wide range of topics on Iranian life and culture as well, past and present. It represents an immense body of scholarship, and references from the entries in it are invaluable to guide further reading. (It is the equivalent in Zoroastrian scholarship of the Stanford Encyclopedia of Philosophy for contemporary Anglo-American philosophers.)

The other incredibly valuable resource is the 'Avesta ~ Zoroastrian Archives' (www.avesta.org), containing a wide range of Zoroastrian sacred texts in their original languages and in English translation. As well as providing accessible texts to scholars, this website is valuable for Zoroastrians seeking to learn more about their tradition and religious writings.

For those with no exposure to Zoroastrianism, a useful general introduction to Zoroastrianism and its history is:

Rose, J. (2011). *Zoroastrianism: An Introduction*. London: I.B. Tauris.

For a deeper dive into Zoroastrian history, a trilogy of books which set the framework for contemporary studies is the following:

Boyce, M. (1975). *A History of Zoroastrianism, Volume 1, Early Period*. Leiden: Brill.
Boyce, M. (1982). *A History of Zoroastrianism, Volume 2, Under the Achaemenians*. Leiden: Brill.
Boyce, M. and Grenet, F. (1991). *A History of Zoroastrianism, Volume 3, Zoroastrianism under Macedonian and Roman Rule*. Leiden: Brill.

And for a more recent overview of contemporary scholarship on Zoroastrianism and its history, I recommend:

Stausberg, M., Veviana, Y. S., and Tessman, A. (eds.) (2015). *The Wiley-Blackwell Companion to Zoroastrianism*. London: Wiley-Blackwell.

1.4.2 Zoroastrianism and Contemporary Philosophy

While Zoroastrian thought is understudied in contemporary philosophy, I do not want to give the impression that this Element is the only work attempting to bring Zoroastrian thought into conversation with contemporary questions as posed in Anglo-American philosophy. The following are a few papers in the recent literature that address interesting questions that I have not had room to discuss in this work. As the reader might imagine, the boundaries between philosophy and other disciplines are porous, and the boundaries between contemporary Anglo-American philosophy and other traditions are not clear either. The following discussion is intended to be illustrative of the various kinds of engagement with Zoroastrianism that can be found in contemporary Anglo-American philosophy, rather than exhaustive. I would welcome being contacted about other contemporary philosophical work engaging with Zoroastrianism.

There has been some interest in the history of philosophy about Zoroastrian influence on Western philosophy, and whether figures in Western philosophy have tried to employ the ancient authority of Zarathustra and Zoroastrianism to support their doctrines:

Horky, P. S. (2009). Persian Cosmos and Greek Philosophy: Plato's Associates and the Zoroastrian *Magoi*. *Oxford Studies in Ancient Philosophy*, 37, 47–103.

Vasunia, P. (2007). The Philosophers' Zarathushtra. In C. Tuplin (ed.), *Persian Responses: Political and Cultural Interaction With(in) the Achaemenid Empire*. Swansea: Classical Press of Wales, pp. 237–266.

Some of the nineteenth-century German idealists, particularly Herder and Hegel, saw Zarathustra's teachings as embodying an important advance in human thought about the divine. While the historical assumptions their work has been based on have sometimes been superseded, there is a literature today on the significance of these philosophers' discussions considered in their own right. Two interesting examples engaging with Hegel's discussion are:

Azadpur, M. (2007). Hegel and the Divinity of Light in Zoroastrianism and Islamic Phenomenology. *Classical Bulletin*, 82(2), 227–246.

Stewart, J. (2018). *Hegel's Interpretation of the Religions of the World: The Logic of the Gods*. Oxford: Oxford University Press.

A work that discusses Zoroastrianism's influence on Hegel's philosophy of history, as well as providing an interesting discussion of Zoroastrian political philosophy, is:

Motameni, A. R. (2014). *Iranian Philosophy of Religion and the History of Political Thought*. UC Riverside Electronic Theses and Dissertations. https://escholarship.org/uc/item/8t2507mw (Accessed 5 November 2024).

Famously, or perhaps infamously, Friedrich Nietzsche employed the prophet Zarathustra in one of his influential philosophical works, *Also Sprach Zarathustra*

(1863–5), as well as others such as *Ecce Homo*. Nietzsche's character announced a 'transvaluation of values', a revolution that Nietzsche took to be the counterpart of an ethical revolution he attributed to the historical Zarathustra. Subsequent scholarship has not exactly vindicated Nietzsche's interpretation of the historical Zarathustra's teachings. Still, some contemporary work has found it useful to compare Nietzsche's character Zarathustra with the historical Zarathustra's teachings. Two illustrative papers exploring these connections are:

> Hassan, P. (2021). Nietzsche's Genealogical Critique and the Historical Zarathustra. *Ergo*, 7(24), 626–658.
> Mariani, E. E. (2020). Nietzsche und die Worte des Avestā. Lektürespuren parsischer Texte in Also Sprach Zarathustra. *Nietzsche Studien*, 49(1), 276–291.

There has been interest in the philosophy of religion about whether Zoroastrianism counts as theologically 'dualist', and whether there are advantages or disadvantages in addressing philosophical puzzles if it is. Papers discussing this include:

> Boyd, J. W. and Crosby, D. A. (1979). Is Zoroastrianism Dualistic or Monotheistic?. *Journal of the American Academy of Religion*, 47(4), 557–588.
> Kronen, J. D. and Menssen, S. (2010). The Defensibility of Zoroastrian Dualism. *Religious Studies*, 46(2), 185–205.

While Zoroastrianism contains a rich set of ethical teachings, it is rarely brought into conversation with contemporary moral and ethical discussion in Anglo-American philosophy. One welcome recent exception is:

> Otto, R. (2021). Zoroaster and the Animals. *Journal of Animal Ethics*, 11(2), 73–82.

Finally, there is an aspect of Zoroastrian thought that I have engaged with and I hope to engage with further. Zoroastrianism is first and foremost a religion, with a set of ritual practices, expectations for adherents, and theological doctrines. But it is possible to read some of the Zoroastrian texts about Ahura Mazda, Angra Mainyu, and their relationship to the world in a cosmological way. Read this way, some traditional Zoroastrian texts offer an account of how the world is made up, and how the variety of things we encounter are due to the operation of a short list of more fundamental principles. I explored one version of this in my paper 'Zurvanist Supersubstantivalism' (Nolan 2023). As I mentioned earlier, the Zurvanist theological account was that Zurvan, associated with time and the chief deity, had as sons Ahura Mazda and Angra Mainyu, the next most powerful deities. To judge from one Greek source (Eudemus of

Rhodes), this received a cosmological interpretation in some quarters, as a theory of the world where the ultimate principle was time, with light and dark, and/or good and evil, as subsidiary principles. I explored the suggestion that we might try to explain everyday objects and processes in terms of that trio of fundamental entities/forces. One thing I thought was interesting in that project is that it suggested options that might be of interest to contemporary people working in metaphysics, for example, about the relationship between time, on the one hand, and ordinary events and objects, on the other.

That project was deliberately limited, but there is evidence that non-Zurvanist Zoroastrians, at various times in the long history of Zoroastrian thought, sought to explain the world in terms of the interaction of light and dark, or of good and evil, or both. (Where this may not just have been a creation story about e.g. the origins being a result of competing creative intentions of Ahura Mazda and Angra Mainyu.) I plan to explore what sort of cosmology or metaphysics we might end up with from these Zoroastrian starting points in future work.

A recent exploration of the history of taking Light and Dark to be fundamental principles, in a Zoroastrian manner, or at least in a manner indebted to Zoroastrian thought, is:

> Meisami, S. (2023). Light/Darkness Dualism and Islamic Metaphysics in Persianate Context. In M. Rustom (ed.), *Festschrift in Honor of William C. Chittick and Sachiko Murata.* Leiden: Brill, pp. 371–388.

2 Zoroastrianism and the Problems of Evil and Suffering

2.1 Introduction to the Problems of Evil and Suffering

The problem of evil and the related problem of suffering are evergreen topics in the philosophy of religion, and for good reason. Many religions are committed to there being very good, very powerful deities that are concerned for our welfare. But a lot of evil and suffering occur, including a lot that the gods apparently dislike, and in some traditions even tell us to do what we can to stop. Why do bad things happen to good people? Why do bad things happen at all, if there are deities powerful enough to prevent them who want them to not happen? This is not just an idle puzzle: many have felt abandoned or betrayed when they suffer greatly and the deities they invoke apparently do nothing.

The problem is sharpened for so-called classical theism. According to classical theism, there is a god who exists, is all powerful and all good. One influential statement of the problem that traces back at least to Mackie 1982, pp. 150–151 adds three other premises: that there is evil, that an omnipotent being could prevent all evil in the world, and finally that an all-good, or omnibenevolent, being, would prevent as much evil, on balance, as it could. These six claims (God's existence, God's omnipotence, God's omnibenevolence, the existence of evil, the could-prevent claim, and the would-prevent claim) are jointly inconsistent. We are under pressure to reject at least one of them.

A variant of this argument can also be run for suffering. It is also plausible that there is suffering in the world; that an omnipotent being could prevent all suffering, and that an omnibenevolent being would prevent as much on-balance suffering as it could. Again, we can see the conflict between the relevant six premises, and something has to go.

Atheists such as Mackie have argued that the most plausible resolution to our dilemma (sexi-lemma?) is that there is no such god. Contemporary theists addressing this problem in the Anglo-American tradition have tended to deny that an all-good god would eliminate all evil and eliminate all suffering, even if she were omnipotent. It is often suggested that there is a *better outcome*, all things considered, if some evil is permitted. Perhaps the best world contains infinite variety, so some evil and suffering make for a better overall tapestry. Perhaps even an omnipotent being cannot allow free will and ensure no evildoing results, and so her best option is to leave her creatures free even when this results in evil. Perhaps a world with suffering and virtuous responses to it is better than any world with no suffering. (Though given the choice between a considerately and skilfully treated cancer, and no cancer in the first place, I would choose to have no cancer.) Or perhaps even an omnipotent being who is all good would permit evil, for reasons that are a mystery to us.

While denying the existence of gods, on the one hand, or explaining why even an omnipotent and omnibenevolent god would allow evil and suffering, perhaps including the evil and suffering we encounter, on the other hand, are of course not the only options. Denying any of the six claims that yield the inconsistent set can be tried, and has been by one theorist or another. (Denying that there *is* any evil or suffering is a surprisingly popular minority view, for example: though it does seem pretty clear to me that there is some suffering in the world, or something enough like suffering that good people often should alleviate it.)

Some theists treat the problem of evil as a non-problem, or a problem that only arises for those who lack sufficient faith. This seems to me to be an error – whether the six premises are jointly inconsistent or not does not seem to be a matter of how much faith anyone has, and rejecting one of them seems not just compatible with theism but not even in tension with being a devout theist.

Even once the so-called logical problems of evil and suffering are disposed of by a theist, there remain related problems that may trouble him. For a set of religious doctrines to be plausible, they should not just be coherent but meet some more demanding standard. (There are all sorts of foolish takes on the world which are internally coherent, even if they fly in the face of evidence or common sense.) Even those convinced that in principle the god of classical theism could permit some evil in the world might struggle to understand how certain kinds of evil and suffering were ever permitted or remain in the world. And even if we deny one of the set of six claims, what replaces it should itself stand up to the evidence about the extent and severity of evil and suffering in the world. Whatever gods there are, the Black Death ravaged the world for centuries, ending millions of lives in torment, including all kinds of people from the most innocent children to the most holy worshippers. Most theists are on the hook for thinking that either their gods allowed that to happen, or lacked the ability to stop it. This can be puzzling, or even confronting, even if the gods of a tradition are not omnipotent, not omnibenevolent, nor even committed to preventing all sorts of evils or all sorts of suffering. You might have expected any being powerful enough to prevent the Black Death in an area and concerned enough about human welfare to prevent the awful deaths involved to have stepped in: but nobody and nothing prevented what happened. (You can, if you like, think that various divinities stopped the plague being even worse.)

Zarathustra described Ahura Mazda as good and as the source of goodness, while the later tradition embraces the claim that he is entirely good. The Zoroastrian tradition is unanimous, as far as I have been able to discover, in holding that Ahura Mazda has great power, and is opposed to evil and the suffering that results from it. So it is no surprise that the Zoroastrian tradition offers material to respond to the question of why we experience evil and suffering nevertheless. One of the Zoroastrian responses is familiar, though I will suggest that there is also another response that can be found in Zoroastrian texts that allows for a distinct, and distinctive, approach to the problem. I do not want to suggest at all that these are the *only* two responses a Zoroastrian might have to the problems of evil and suffering. Much of the Zoroastrian tradition stresses the importance of free will and people freely choosing between good and evil, so various forms of the so-called free-will defence might appeal to some Zoroastrians. (Influential discussions of the free-will defence include Rowe 1979, Plantinga 1974, Swinburne 1998, and Lewis 1993.) I focus on the two below because they strike me as the most distinctively Zoroastrian responses, though as I will discuss options like these are available for many non-Zoroastrian theists as well.

Part of one potential Zoroastrian response is well known, and serves to undercut the logical problems of evil and suffering as stated in the beginning of the section. Historically, many Zoroastrian texts present the present state of the world as the site of a struggle between the forces of good, headed by the all-good god Ahura Mazda (/Ormazd), and the forces of evil, headed by Angra Mainyu (/Ahriman). This struggle is for the highest stakes: control of the world and everything in it. Zoroastrianism's founding prophet Zarathustra had revealed to him that Ahura Mazda and the forces of good will eventually win, and the later Zoroastrian tradition suggests that on the day of victory evil will be eliminated and Angra Mainyu himself will be destroyed or rendered harmless.

So far this can sound like the contest presented by some Christian and Muslim writings between the forces of good and the forces of evil, the former headed by God and the latter headed by the Devil, or Satan. Where Zoroastrianism has sometimes diverged from this Abrahamic tradition is that Angra Mainyu is often presented as an independent force, not created by Ahura Mazda, and not subject to Ahura Mazda's will, in the near-term at least. A natural inference from the picture of Ahura Mazda and Angra Mainyu, or Ormazd and Ahriman, as independent and contending forces is that Ahura Mazda, while being the most powerful of all, is not omnipotent. He is seeking to vanquish Angra Mainyu, and will eventually, but Ahura Mazda has not driven evil out of the world yet because he cannot, due to Angra Mainyu's opposition. One way to take this tradition is that Ahura Mazda is all-good, but the evil that we find in the world is because this is no mock-battle with Angra Mainyu: Ahura Mazda will win when he can. In some presentations, it sounds as if it would have been best if Ahura Mazda had won an instant victory: the explanation for Ahura Mazda's not doing this is not that he somehow chose a worse option over a better, but rather that Angra Mainyu could not be overcome so easily.

If Ahura Mazda is not omnipotent, and is faced with powerful evil opposition, we can explain how it is that he is perfectly good and yet there is widespread evil and suffering in the world. Even if he has the power to intervene to stop various particular evils, he faces a powerful and determined enemy who is promoting evil, and the suffering that goes along with it. (Ahura Mazda has many assistants, including many good people, but Angra Mainyu has many allies as well, including, perhaps unwittingly, many evil and flawed people.) Questions may remain about what exactly Ahura Mazda's tactics are and why various good or evil things happen in the world, but the overall shape of this doctrine is clear enough. Evil things happen because of Angra Mainyu's activities, and Ahura Mazda is doing his best to bring all of this evil to an end. (Zoroastrian eschatology envisages a state where evil has been completely removed from the world (e.g. Denkard 7.11 (Sanjana 1876), Bundahishn 34: 18–33 (Agostini and Thrope 2020, pp. 181–182), and see Section 3.2) which suggests Ahura Mazda would eliminate all the evil he could, since he *will* eliminate all evil when he can.)

I should note that this picture of Ahura Mazda and Angra Mainyu as independent warring powers is not universal among Zoroastrian communities. Some Parsi communities hold that, properly interpreted, there is no such being as Angra Mainyu/Ahriman at all: either evil is only a privation or mirage, or while there is evil in the world it is in no sense a personal force or associated with a supernatural being. See, for example, the discussion of nineteenth-century Parsi views in Maneck 1997 chapter 8. Other Zoroastrian traditions hold that Angra Mainyu and the other powers of evil are creations of Ahura Mazda and subject to him, a position more like the (stereotypically) Christian position where Satan is one of God's creatures and just as subject to God's will as any other subsidiary being. On this latter conception, there may not be any sense in which Ahura Mazda fails to be omnipotent, and Angra Mainyu's actions are subject, at least in theory, to Ahura Mazda's allowing Angra Mainyu to act. In one version, Ahura Mazda creates both Angra Mainyu and the greatest of Ahura Mazda's servants, Spenta Mainyu ('good spirit'). He then sets these two spirits to struggle against each other, but presumably subject to Ahura Mazda's permissive will.

An interesting strand of Zoroastrian strand of thought which takes Ahura Mazda to be omnipotent is to be found in the ninth century *Doubt-Removing Book of Mardanfarrox* (Mardānfarrox 2015). The author asserts that Ahura Mazda is all-powerful (1.1, p. 29), but when he explicitly turns to the question of why Ahura Mazda does not prevent Angra Mainyu's evil, Mardanfarrox asserts that not even Ahura Mazda could prevent Angra Mainyu from being evil, since Angra Mainyu is essentially evil, and not even omnipotence requires being able to do the impossible (3.1–15, pp. 46–49). Mardanfarrox does go on to say that Ahura Mazda can limit Angra Mainyu, as a farmer traps a pest in a net or trap (4.63–80, pp. 63–64). There are two puzzling things about this response to the problem of why Ahura Mazda does not prevent all evil. One is the suggestion that even omnipotent Ahura Mazda cannot destroy Angra Mainyu (since even if Angra Mainyu is essentially evil, that does not by itself suggest he is indestructible), and the other is that Mardanfarrox has not provided an explanation of why Ahura Mazda did not immediately remove Angra Mainyu's ability to harm anything else. A farmer may have to wear down a beast for a period of time before capturing it, but presumably omnipotence does not come with such a limitation. Still, we can extract from Mardanfarrox's discussion an intermediate position: there is some evil that not even omnipotence can prevent, but there is other evil that omnipotence can (but has not yet for reasons not explained by Mardanfarrox, at least not in these passages).

Views on which Ahura Mazda is omnipotent and could effortlessly eliminate *all* evil if he chose may find it much harder to explain the presence of evil despite Ahura Mazda's omnibenevolence. They may be well advised to try a different response, such as the appeal to the value of free will discussed earlier (Angra Mainyu's or the free will of human beings tempted by evil), or perhaps even the merit theodicy discussed later in this section.

One version of Zoroastrianism that did clearly maintain that Angra Mainyu is a distinct power, not derivative of Ahura Mazda and in a struggle with him that has lasted as long as the material world has, was Zurvanism. (See Section 1.2.) According to Zurvanism, Ahura Mazda and Angra Mainyu were the 'twins' Zarathustra describes in *Yasna* 30:3. Their father was Zurvan, who is a god of time or infinite time. In some versions of Zurvanism it is Zurvan who sets the stage for the twins to battle, perhaps by creating the material world, and seems to act as some sort of enforcer of the rules of the struggle. The Zurvanist picture, at least, suggests that Ahura Mazda is not omnipotent, and is doing his best against Angra Mainyu while facing a genuine challenge. One puzzle about Zurvanism is whether *Zurvan* is supposed to be omnipotent, and whether there is a problem of evil or suffering about why there is evil given that *Zurvan* could prevent it. Even if Zurvan is intended to be all-powerful, I see no evidence in the surviving stories that Zurvan is conceived of as all-good. He has some preference for Ahura Mazda, but perhaps his motives are other than the wholly good ones of Ahura Mazda.

Zurvanism does not seem to be the only strand of Zoroastrian thought that characterises Angra Mainyu as an opponent that Ahura Mazda does not control. The idea that Angra Mainyu is an independent being draws some support from creation stories which do not have Ahura Mazda creating Angra Mainyu but rather Ahura Mazda being aware of Angra Mainyu's existence before any creative act (Greater Bundahishn 0–12, Agostini and Thrope 2020, p. 6), and some support from the argument made in several places that Ahura Mazda is not responsible for the creation of any evil (to be discussed soon): this seems to require that Ahura Mazda not be the creator of the chief evil being, especially since Angra Mainyu is even described as essentially evil in some Zoroastrian texts (e.g. Mardānfarrox 2015, p. 29).

I do not want to take a stand on whether Zoroastrians *should* think Angra Mainyu/Ahriman is a power independent of Ahura Mazda, or even whether they should take talk of Angra Mainyu as being literally about a powerful evil being at all. Instead, my concern is to examine the appeal of the view that Ahura Mazda is limited by Angra Mainyu and his actions. I will argue that it offers *one* satisfying response to the problems of evil and suffering that began this section.

One appealing thing about the types of Zoroastrianism that see Angra Mainyu as a genuine enemy who Ahura Mazda must struggle to defeat is that it gives good human beings a more significant role in the cosmos. Ahura Mazda is receiving help in a genuine task, and even though our contributions are dwarfed by his we are jointly saving the world. This is less so in some Jewish, Christian, and Islamic traditions where God could end all evil and banish all suffering with less effort than it takes us to breathe, but chooses not to for various purposes of his own. Traditions according to which evil is something God himself has created, or even exists only through his 'permissive will', tend to make evil into another one of God's tools rather than a phenomenon in the world opposed to, and rejected absolutely by, the good deity. The Ulema i-Islam (Dhabhar 1932, pp. 439–440) seems to offer as an objection to Islam, and by extension Christianity and Judaism, that *they* think the all-good god is responsible for evils as well as good, and there even seems to be the suggestion that a god whose creation is evil is itself to that extent evil (Dhabhar 1932, p. 445). The Zoroastrian author of this text treats the suggestion that the good god is responsible for all evils as impious as well as false. Mardānfarrox 2015 also relies on this objection to Judaism, Islam, and arguably Christiantity.

As well as the problem of explaining why there is any evil at all, there are also problems of explaining why there are various kinds of evil. One of the most famous of these is the problem of *natural evil* (or natural suffering). Some evil or suffering does not seem to flow from the actions of intelligent agents besides God: in one influential presentation (Rowe 1979), we are asked about the experience of wild animals burning to death in forest fires before humans even appear on the Earth. It would be surprising if any of us were responsible for that, or that it would somehow be the price of free action. Zoroastrians have a straightforward response to the apparent problem of natural evil (/natural suffering) as well. *All* the suffering and imperfections in the world are due to Angra Mainyu and his minions: he is responsible, directly or indirectly, for bad things and suffering that happens even when no humans are around.

Likewise, for specific problems such as the existence of *horrendous* evils. Some responses to the problem of evil give us a sense of why an all-good deity would allow for some evils: perhaps they build character, or test us. But some evils seem disproportionately bad to achieve those aims. People being tortured to death, children being killed in front of their parents, the Atlantic slave trade, all seem like horrors out of proportion to the supposed need for people to have something to make some morally significant choices about, or to have morally significant projects. But Angra Mainyu is certainly malevolent enough to aim for things that bad, and depending on the details of the great struggle Ahura Mazda cannot stop all of Angra Mainyu's influence all the time. We might be curious about how the details are supposed to work, but the general picture is consistent with the forces of evil producing catastrophic outcomes on occasion.

Zoroastrianism even has a reasonable response to the question of why there is *so much* evil or suffering in the world. Some responses to the problem of evil attempt to explain why God each of us might face some amount of suffering or even wrong-doing in the world, to build character, or provide contrast, or for various other purposes. But even apart from the intensity of horrendous evils, the sheer scale of evil in our world looks badly calibrated to be just enough for the alleged benefits that flow from it. Take the life of someone who faces very little in the way of challenges, or faces challenges they overcome with good cheer. Why not inflict the level of evil that person suffers as the amount to subject everyone to, rather than the levels we encounter? On the picture where Ahriman is a powerful force in his own right, this high level of evil and suffering might be unpreventable by Ahura Mazda and the forces of good, or at least unpreventable without paying some higher cost elsewhere. An active and independent evil principle, if a powerful enough one is postulated, might be a better explanation of grave evil in the world than the model of a benevolent parent giving His children terminal bone cancer to teach them a lesson.

An explanation of evil that appeals to the limits of an omnibenevolent deity is fairly straightforward, especially if we posit sufficiently powerful beings or forces that would produce evil outcomes. This explanation for evil is unavailable to some Zoroastrians who think that Ahura Mazda is omnipotent: they must look elsewhere for why he permits the material world to contain so many states which he apparently detests. This is one reason to explore other Zoroastrian responses to the problem of evil. Another reason is that not all responses to the problem of evil are in competition: it is consistent to reject *more than one* of the six premises that produce the classic problem, and even Zoroastrians who do not think Ahura Mazda is all powerful may think that even if he were, he would permit some evils for some important purpose (i.e. they would deny the claim that an omnibenevolent being would eliminate all the evils they could).

Many attempted explanations of why an all-good, all-powerful being would allow evil founder on the problem that an all-powerful being could plausibly take shortcuts that would produce the benefit without the pain. A surgeon may have to cause injury and subsequent pain to, for example, remove a bullet from an injured soldier. But an omnipotent being could presumably patch a soldier up as good as new without any surgical wounds or subsequent discomfort. The most promising stories about why an omnibenevolent, omnipotent being would permit some evils offer a story about why it would be *impossible* to have the benefit being pursued without the evil being allowed: cases where not even omnipotence would allow one to have one's cake and eat it too.

One kind of response to the problems of evil and suffering, as mentioned earlier, is a free-will defence, according to which not even an omnipotent, omnibenevolent being could *ensure* the absence of evil and suffering if the benefits of having free-created beings are to be secured. While that will be an approach appealing to some Zoroastrians, since it is a relatively well-explored avenue of response I will focus on a third, distinctively Zoroastrian, option for explaining Ahura Mazda's permitting of evil, in terms of a good that not even an omnipotent being could secure without there being some evil.

2.2 Paradise and Merit

Many of these features of Zoroastrianism, or other dualist responses to the problem of evil and suffering, are well enough known in the literature. However, there is at least one other distinctive justification for permitting evils and suffering in the world as we find it found in Zoroastrian texts. This justification, on the face of it, would explain why even an omnipotent, all-good being would permit evil and suffering. It may be of especial use to Zoroastrians who think Ahura Mazda is omnipotent after all, or is at least powerful enough to bring Angra Mainyu and his works to an end whenever Ahura Mazda wishes. On the other hand, Zoroastrians who wish to maintain that Ahura Mazda is not omnipotent (or at least is not omnipotent *yet*, since the limits of his power may be removed once evil is destroyed) may still be interested in a justification for some current evil and suffering that would remain even if we decided Ahura Mazda is omnipotent after all. The two explanations of evil and suffering need not be in tension.[1]

Several passages of important Zoroastrian texts deal with what the experience of a righteous person will be after they die. Several of these passages stress the value of the good deeds and righteousness of the saved. In the Menog i-Khrad II:125–139 (West 1885, pp. 19–20), for example, the soul is met by a beautiful woman who personifies the righteous deeds, or *dēn,* performed by the person in life. And evildoers are met by an ugly and frightening woman representing the evil they have done (Menog i-Khrad II: 167–171, West 1885, pp. 23–24). Someone's *dēn* can also be, in this context, their conscience or the moral aspect of their spirit, or their righteousness, or perhaps even their wisdom concerning moral matters. Whatever exactly they are confronted with, it is closely connected with their character and good deeds in their earthly life, and the value of these for the righteous, or the disvalue of these for the wicked, is an important part of what they take with them into the afterlife. I will take the relevant feature they bring into the afterlife to be 'merit' in what follows, though some may prefer a different term for how a person's *dēn* in this life might appropriately influence their afterlife.

The future existence of good people involves their being in heaven, though this heavenly state is described differently in different places. The overall impression is that there is a spiritual heavenly state that begins soon after death, followed by the resurrection of the body in the final stages of the battle against evil, when the material world will be restored. What these depictions share, however, is the conviction that there is a wonderful state that will last forever for the righteous,

---

[1] There might be a tension about whether Ahura Mazda would eliminate *all* evil immediately if he could, given the merit defence: but one could hold that Ahura Mazda lacks the power to immediately end all evil, *and* even if he could, he would leave some amount around for a finite time: presumably a relatively small amount compared to the evil we find in the world.

and that it is a valuable state to be in: it is a reward, it lacks pain and loss and fear, and is blissful. You might naturally think that an eternity where every day is very good is infinitely valuable, even if each day-length of time is finitely good. Even if eternal heaven is infinitely valuable, though, some outcomes of infinite value may be better than others. (Compare spending an eternity in heaven vs every tenth day in heaven and the other nine being humdrum and only mildly pleasant.)

It is not clear how to model different levels of good when all the levels are infinitely greater than a finite good. If we just measure units of good with ordinary numbers, we will not assign any outcome an infinite value, and if we use an additional infinite value, for example, corresponding to the 'countable infinite' aleph-zero, then adding to it, subtracting from it, or multiplying it by any non-zero finite amount will leave it unchanged. There are, however, various proposals about how to represent different levels of infinite value in the literature: see Mulgan 2002, Lauwers and Vallentyne 2004, and Chen and Rubio 2020 for some proposals. I will not develop or defend any particular account of how to handle differing infinite values here, but I will take for granted that somehow or other we can vindicate the thought that there are different possible infinite amounts of value, some greater than others, and that it makes sense for an omnibenevolent being to prefer higher infinite levels of value to lower levels.

Perhaps experiencing infinite blissful life *as an appropriate reward* is even more valuable than it would be for someone who, for example, always experiences heaven without any opportunity to earn or deserve it. It would be difficult to quantify how much better: if one day of merited bliss is finitely better than one day of bliss that has not been merited, an infinity of days of merited bliss may well be infinitely better than an infinity days of not-merited bliss. As mentioned in Section 2, we would need a way to compare better and worse infinite futures even when all of them are infinitely good. Provided the benefit of an eternity of merited reward is high enough, however, it could make the package of infinite merited bliss plus finite troubles in this life be more choice-worthy than infinite non-merited bliss without any initial suffering. Not that we finite beings are offered that choice, but it is perhaps one an omnibenevolent being would make on our behalf, given those options.

One thing that is interesting about this merit approach is that merit for past deeds is not something that is entirely intrinsic to a person who has it. Not even omnipotence could create a person from scratch who comes with merit for past deeds unless that person has in fact done those deeds. (Or perhaps has that merit transferred from someone who earned it directly.) So we have the makings of a story about why an omnipotent being would allow evil for a sake of good, rather than just producing the good directly via an exercise of infinite power. On this picture, even if Ahura Mazda were omnipotent, he would not just give every good being infinite bliss straight away. It would be even better to have them struggle against and overcome some evil and suffering, so the infinite bliss would be *even better* by being a merited reward, and it would be so much better as to make up for whatever finite levels of evil and suffering there are before our rewards.

This arguably makes this 'merit defence' superior to other attempts to justify evils and suffering by reference to goods that are produced. The greatest challenge many of these approaches face is explaining why the evil is a conceptually or logically necessary precondition of the consequent good, in a way that not even an omnipotent being could circumvent. Two prominent attempts in the twentieth-century Anglo-American tradition to specify goods that make evil and suffering worthwhile, and which could not be secured without evil and suffering, are the 'higher order goods' approach discussed by John Mackie 1982, pp. 153–155 and the 'Soul-making theodicy' advanced by John Hick (Hick 1978). In both cases, goods are involved that would be worth some evil or suffering if that was the only way to get them. But in both cases, these responses to the problem of evil need to make plausible that even an omnipotent being could not produce the good without the evil.

Mackie discusses the suggestion that evils might be required for some goods: 'higher order' goods such as courageous or self-sacrificing responses to evil and suffering, for example. (Or for that matter the aesthetic value of a varied world: there are various options, provided the evil or suffering is not just a cause of the subsequent good, but somehow partially constitutes it or is a strictly necessary condition for it.) Mackie suggests that these responses can only justify the existence of evils or suffering that are required for these further goods, and so fails to explain the full range of evils and suffering we observe, many of which do not seem absolutely needed for actual goods that have evils or suffering as prerequisites. Beyond Mackie's own objection, there is also the problem for these higher-order goods theodicies of explaining why the substitutes without any evil are so inferior. A world can have variety in it without containing bone-cancer, a heroic response can be launched even to a false-alarm, and so on.

Hick 1978 stresses the need for 'soul-making'. On his view, it is very valuable for beings to autonomously shape their souls through important decisions, and a central part of this importance is that beings should *freely* grow towards God. The value of this autonomous self-creation in the face of adversity is so great that an omnipotent and omnibenevolent being could allow there to be suffering and other challenges that face beings like us, to give us an environment conducive to our soul-making. The evils and suffering we face would be allowed by even an all-powerful and all-good god to put us in a position to forge our own characters and selves.

Let us allow, at least for the sake of the argument, that the sort of complex and autonomous souls that are the outcome of the process are especially valuable. One puzzle in the case of soul-making is why it is meant to be additionally valuable to be the author of one's own state of the soul. We should not answer that this is the only way complex and valuable souls can be brought into existence, on pain of compromising divine omnipotence. If God values complex and unique souls, he could bring them into existence already fully formed, presumably. Hick's answer appears to be that the souls that result from this procedure are more valuable through having been self-created *autonomously*. If Hick wished to argue that God could not ensure autonomous or free growth of the right sort without at least risking evil and suffering, his account might need to draw on the sorts of controversial resources offered by free-will explanations of the existence of evil and suffering.

Another puzzle is why autonomous soul-making *necessarily* involves suffering and the infliction of evil. Consider an unformed angel creatively selecting the characteristics of their soul, like the character-creation stage of a roleplaying game. They end up with an intricately complex, original, nuanced character, with plenty of virtues and resilience, but without suffering any harm or distress in the process. (They may have been obliged to give up some desirable qualities in favour of others, but this need not cause any distress.) If it is possible to create oneself and develop a desirable kind of soul by some means other than experiencing evils and suffering, and it only needs to be possible in the sense that an omnipotent being could enable it to happen, then requiring us to forge our souls in a crucible of torment and death would again be undermotivated. While Hick's approach has supporters, without good answers to these challenges it does not get very far in making plausible that an all-good god would choose, or even allow, the kinds of evils and suffering that we face.

So far I have been suggesting that the bliss being *merited* rather than unmerited makes it more valuable. A slightly different alternative is to say that merit does not modify the value of the bliss, but instead, it is just a good thing to have on its own, so the best of afterlives consists in infinite bliss *plus* merit. Or we could think that it is not just having merit, but knowing one has merit that is so valuable. That warm feeling you get when you realise you helped someone or did something else good may be especially valuable when it goes along with genuine merit, for example. All these variants keep the feature that having genuine merit for overcoming evil is something that it is impossible to have without there being evil that has been overcome: not even an omnipotent being can pop someone into existence with this sort of merit, no matter how warm and fuzzy that person might feel inside, or how much the person *would* oppose evil if given the opportunity.

2.3 Remaining Challenges

No doubt a range of reasons could be offered to find this 'merit' solution to the problems of evil and suffering unsatisfactory. After all, there is a vast literature back-and-forth about problems of evil and suffering as they arise in Christian, Jewish, and Islamic settings. I will discuss here three of the most serious challenges I can see for the justification of evil and suffering by the appeal to merit I have outlined previously.

The first challenge is that on the face of it, there is suffering in the world that is not due to fighting evil. All sorts of maladies and inconveniences and injuries can occur in life, and not all of them particularly have much to do with a struggle against evil or any larger plan. These range from minor events (cutting my finger making lunch) to dramatic (a freak rockslide killing dozens, or the Chixilub asteroid eliminating entire species and causing the painful deaths of many thousands of animals). These harms are not on the face of it part of the struggle against evil, nor are they evils that we meritoriously struggle against. It is true that I put an effort into not cutting my finger when cutting tomatoes, and treat my finger when I do slip, but I doubt either of those activities would place me among the meritorious in an afterlife.

Here the cosmic nature of the forces of evil in the Zoroastrian picture might make a difference. It is true that my cutting my finger while making a sandwich is not very significant in the scheme of things. But we live in a world where we are subject to injuries and pain and the like because of the intermingling of Angra Mainyu's influence and that of his cohorts. When they are defeated, there will be no more injuries and threats and pain, and it is the struggle against this whole intermixture of evil in the world that is the source of merit. So many of these evils and sources of suffering are manifestations of the evil to be struggled against, according to a standard Zoroastrian picture, and the struggle against Angra Mainyu and his minions that we engage in when we engage in good thoughts, good words, and good deeds, or which Zoroastrians advance by engaging in the relevant rituals, counts as working to overcome everything from kitchen accidents to traffic gridlock to influenza in wild bird populations. It may be a surprising view that everything that causes pain or evil can be meritoriously combatted and resisted, but it is not an indefensible one.

Another challenge to this picture of evil and suffering being justified by merit accrued in fighting evil is that there are *failures* to fight evil and earn merit. Suppose I endure oppression, but when faced with an effective opportunity to end that oppression through righteous struggle I take a pass, because I am cowed, or because I am lazy or inattentive, or because it would compromise opportunities to engage in oppression of my own. I still suffer from the oppression I endure, let us allow. And I do not incur much merit as a result, since I do not do the standing up to evil that would be desirable. There are many cases where people suffer as part of a potential struggle against evil, but they do not end up performing that struggle. (Another case would be e.g. feeling the pangs of temptation, and then giving in to that temptation. The pangs are unpleasant, but are not worth it for resulting merit in this case.) Even if we allow that some evil is worth it because of the good that results from meritorious struggle against it, other evil does not seem to be compensated for in this way. A particularly stark case, in some Zoroastrian eschatologies, is the evil that happens to those who end up damned. The evil they endure is not a constitutive means to any merited bliss in an afterlife, at least according to understandings where the damned are not eventually saved after their suffering in the afterlife.

I think this problem is one of the most serious for the merit defence, considered in isolation. A Zoroastrian could hold that in fact every evil or harm *does* form the basis of an accrual of merit to someone: perhaps even if Alexander is an evildoer who gives in to evil rather than resists it, others struggling against him, or trying to save him, gain merit indirectly from the evil he faces but does not resist. Even the damned, according to some Zoroastrian accounts of the afterlife, suffer a finite punishment before eternal happiness, so perhaps even their redeeming results in some merit, whether that merit is theirs or other agents. But I suspect when addressing this problem Zoroastrians are best off combining the merit defence with other available accounts of why there is evil in Ahura Mazda's cosmos. An appeal to a lack of omnipotence for example: perhaps it lies beyond Ahura Mazda's current powers to fine-tune the presentation of evil so that it appears only when it would be meritoriously resisted or overcome. Or perhaps an appeal to a free-will defence is needed: perhaps the best even an omnipotent being can do is allow free creatures to be confronted with evil, thus giving them a reasonable opportunity to respond meritoriously, without being able to *ensure* that they freely choose to react to that evil in a meritorious way. The goodness of the acquisition of merit might be part of the story about why a good deity would allow evil, even if it ends up not being able to be the whole story.

A third challenge is to the claim that the struggle against evil is *necessary* for the merit that makes eternal bliss even better, or makes salvation a *reward* and not just a gift. If there were some easier or less damaging way to ensure the same good accrued to the saved, we would not yet have shown that an all-good God would pick this method for ensuring the admittedly great good produced. If merit or desert was some internal quantity like a spiritual halo, for example, the saved could just be filled up with merit or desert as part of the process of admitting them to heaven, without the messy and tragic costs that come with struggling against evil.

Here, I think Zoroastrians have something plausible to say about why even an omnipotent being could not just fill creatures up with merit or desert. It does not even seem possible that someone could earn merit for something that nobody did, or be rewarded without something happening to create desert for a reward. Of course, people could receive medals or cash prizes or praise 'out of the blue' with nothing relevant before those happenings, but that would not mean those prizes, and so on were genuinely rewards or genuinely merited. Merit is not something that can just be varied independently of actions or character, even by omnipotent beings. (This is assuming, as is common, that not even omnipotent beings can do the conceptually or metaphysically impossible.)

Those interested in the 'merit defence' would also need to explain why merit or reward could not be earned through something less drastic than facing evil and suffering. Perhaps some bestowed good is not a *reward* if it is not in response to anything the recipient (or people associated with the recipient) has done. Not even an omnipotent being can create purely reward-worthy creatures when nothing has been done to deserve reward, let us allow. But we normally think rewards can be merited in a range of ways. If I do something especially good for someone else, or I create something especially valuable, or I assist or encourage some good act, then that might accrue some merit or result in me having some desert. But acts like that could plausibly happen in worlds where there is no evil. A choir of angels each creating a new wonderful song, and being rewarded for it, does not, on the face of it, involve any evil or suffering. I suspect the best thing for a defender of the merit defence to say about this problem is that while good acts in the absence of evil might be meritorious, there is a certain kind of especially valuable merit that only comes from opposing evil or suffering for good. Someone in heaven looking back at their successful traversal of the vale of tears, and the advance they contributed to in the perfection of the whole world, has a significantly better eternity of bliss, because it is merited to such a high degree, compared to a hypothetical person who 'earned' their eternity of bliss only by engaging in painless and pleasant creative activity.

A fourth challenge is whether it is plausible that there is an *optimal amount* of opportunity for the acquisition of merit. Some may well earn more merit than others through their actions: that is the result of their choices, and maybe it has to be a result of their free choices in order to be merit-worthy in the first place. But it is not up to us what our opportunities to earn merit are, and some seem to have many fewer opportunities for that than others. An uneducated person in a pre-modern small island community might have no opportunity to be a great philanthropist, a heroic medical researcher or a war hero, especially if they are born with serious disabilities. If a child with few opportunities to gain merit dies and goes to heaven they will still have a high balance of good over evil in their existence, but it seems less than optimific that they missed out on most of the opportunities to make their afterlife even better (infinitely better?) in the way that a high degree of merit is supposed to. Surely an omnibenevolent being would do better by the child if the being could.

In response to this challenge, Zoroastrians could point out that all of us are players in the ultimate struggle against evil: in opposing Angra Mainyu and his servants in whatever way we can, we play a role in a cosmic struggle vastly outrunning any mundane struggle against evil empires or dangerous diseases. It is true that some have larger parts in this struggle than others: most Zoroastrians would not compare their own accomplishments with Zarathustra's, for example. But it might be that merit is not earned more by the captains and the heroes than is earned, in principle, by those playing smaller roles: maybe doing the best with what you have is as meritorious whether you have a few people around you to bless with good words and deeds as when you have a whole continent in your care. (Compare Jesus's claim that the widow who gives all she has to charity has 'put in more than all', compared to those who gave much more in monetary terms but a smaller percentage of what they had (Luke 21:1–4).) It is clear Zoroastrians or others pursing a merit theodicy should give this, or some other story, about why the distribution of opportunities for merit does not undermine this explanation of why we are faced with evil and suffering in the proportions we encounter.

A final challenge to this picture is the question of whether it can handle what I will label the *distributive* problem of evil. It is, more or less, the problem highlighted by Adams 1989. Suppose an all-good being allows great evil in order to secure even greater good. There is something uncomfortable about any distribution where the people who undergo the evil are not given any, or much, of the great good. Most of us think that an omnibenevolent being does not just care about ensuring an overall better outcome, but cares about *each* agent: it seems less than ideal, and maybe unjust, that some bear great costs without corresponding benefits while others gain benefits that far outweigh any costs they pay personally. Perhaps an omnibenevolent being with constrained enough options does sometimes sacrifice the few to benefit the many: it is hard to send a soldier to be maimed or killed for her or his country, even if the alternative is defeat and enslavement of an entire group. Still, it is sometimes the right thing to do, when faced with a dangerous enemy, and maybe something even an omnibenevolent leader would do if she had few other options.

If good people secure an infinitely valuable afterlife, but bad people get nothing infinitely good, it is harder to see why it is okay for the second group to undergo suffering or evil as part of the overall plan. This is especially so when those who miss out on infinite good suffer before they have done very much to deserve it. (Consider a child who suffers greatly from the cruelty of others, before turning into a cruel adult who loses their spot in paradise.) Even if suffering and evil are worth it in the long run for those who have an infinitely valuable afterlife boosted by their merit in standing up to life's challenges, it is not yet clear it would be worth it to suffer and be wronged for those not getting that kind of afterlife.

Adams herself suggests that the distributive problem of evil is best responded to with a *universalist* doctrine, according to which everyone is saved and goes to heaven. If each person who suffers evils in their finite lifetime then receives an eternity of heaven, then the benefits that accrue to each person outweigh (and infinitely outweigh) the harms that person suffers.

Interestingly, as we will see in Section 3, universal salvation appears to be part of some Zoroastrian understandings of the afterlife. They can avail themselves of the same sort of solution that Adams suggests. And if everyone in an afterlife of bliss bears some merit for some of the evil and suffering they faced, things might be even better *for them* overall than if they had never faced any evil or suffering. Even if there are some people who deserve *no* merit for their actions, at least the infinite benefit of eternal bliss outweighs any finite harms they bore: perhaps in a case like this an omnibenevolent being could be satisfied that their harm can be outweighed by the benefits merit gives to others, even if the meritless person themselves would have been better off without their own evils and suffering.

My sense is that not all Zoroastrians have been universalists: in Section 3, I will mention some texts that suggest some evil-doers are denied heaven, either through an eternity of hell or through being destroyed altogether when evil is destroyed. In particular, those who take the existence of Angra Mainyu/ Ahriman literally often think at least *he* will be destroyed and not turned into a being of pure good experiencing an eternity of happiness. The destruction of evil *is*, in part, the destruction of Angra Mainyu, in this way of thinking. Zoroastrians who think some people will not receive eternal bliss need another response to the distributive problem of evil.

Fortunately, they have a range of familiar options at this point. Perhaps some version of the free-will defence works here: these people will suffer because of the free choices they have chosen, and it is the cost of having free-willed agents in the first place that some will give in to evil and not see eternal bliss. Or perhaps this is the best Ahura Mazda can do: wars have casualties, and the most he can do, even at the end of time, for the evil is to visit destruction on them. (If Ahura Mazda cannot e.g. redeem Angra Mainyu and make him an entirely good being, that looks like a limitation on Ahura Mazda's power: but remember that

Ahura Mazda might not have unlimited power over evil, which is why this struggle is required in the first place).

2.4 Resources for Other Traditions

Many traditions struggle with coming up with a plausible account of how an all-powerful, all-good deity could or would permit evil and suffering, including serious evils like torture and oppression. In many of these traditions, some at least have explored the idea that God is not omnipotent, but doing his best in difficult circumstances, with some suffering and evildoing being at worst unavoidable and at best an unfortunate tradeoff to prevent worse or bring about goods that, in the circumstances, God cannot bring about without costs.

It seems to me that many of those traditions, at least those who take an afterlife of reward seriously, could employ the idea that an eternity of heaven as a deserved reward for earthly life is much better than an eternity of heaven without reward or desert. If not even an omnipotent being could create a deserved reward without the recipient doing things to deserve it, and if some of those things need to be facing and overcoming evil, we have an account available of why even an omnipotent and omnibenevolent being would allow their creatures to encounter evil before an eternity of heaven.

As previously noted, this justification for God to allow a world with much evil, pain and suffering has some limitations. Evil and suffering that people suffer, but not in the course of the struggle against evil, may need some other explanation. For traditions that see less of the suffering in the world as the work of malign forces may want to hold that resisting or enduring suffering confers merit or desert in some other way. Perhaps living through suffering and loss without total despair, or while retaining faith in God, brings merit even when the suffering does not result from any evil being done. Some traditions will want to decouple the value of heaven from anything to do with merit or desert on the grounds that the whole idea that we could 'deserve' the bounty of God is a mistake. Finally, theological doctrines according to which some people are damned to eternal torment, or even annihilation, will have to find resources elsewhere to answer Adams's distributive problem of evil.

The idea that even an omnipotent omnibenevolent being would allow some evil so that an infinitely good afterlife would be *even better* because of merit need not be the whole story for any theistic tradition seeking to understand why there is evil in the world. It does not rule out other candidate explanations: perhaps even an omnipotent omnibenevolent being would allow some evil, and *in addition* omnibenevolent beings are less than omnipotent, or perhaps there are other good reasons for even omnibenevolent and omnipotent beings to allow some evils. And nothing I have said here has been intended to show that traditions which postulate an omnibenevolent and omnipotent being *need* a rationally satisfying theodicy: some have held that we have no satisfying story about evil being permitted by an omnipotent and omnibenevolent being, but that reflects more on limits to our capacity to understand divinity and evil than any internal problem with the theistic picture itself. Though an intellectually satisfying understanding of the existence of evil and suffering in these frameworks would be a nice thing to have, if it does turn out to be available.

3 Zoroastrianism and Puzzles about Eternal Reward

Many religious traditions teach that there is a life after death, and many teach that there is some kind of heaven or paradise for the saved. This theme is present in Zoroastrianism from very early in its history. In the Gathas, the oldest part of the Zoroastrian sacred books, the great god Ahura Mazda promises Zarathustra that the good will be rewarded with 'health and immortality' (Ys 31.21, Kanga 1997, p. 61), while the wicked will be punished (e.g. Ys 32.6, 32.7, Kanga 1997, pp. 70, 71). Later in the Zoroastrian tradition a series of accounts developed of the last day of the struggle between good and evil: the *frasokereti*. Aided by the final saviour (Sayoshant), Ahura Mazda will bodily resurrect all people who have died, who will face a final test, the good proceeding to an eternal life without suffering and evil in a perfected material realm, while all the evil in the universe will be burned away by a great river of molten metal. As we will see, the tradition is less univocal about what happens to human evildoers and followers of Ahriman and his demons, or *daiwas*. Those who are only a little evil will be purified in the molten metal that destroys all evil, and after this painful purification will also partake in eternal blissful life (*Greater Bundahishn* 34: 18–23). According to some traditions, the evil face an eternity in hell (e.g. the *Menog-i Krad* XL:31, West 1885, p. 81), but in the main tradition, I will consider they are dealt with by the purification process as well. According to some versions, all human beings are purified and saved, and according to another version, the wicked are destroyed along with their evil.

Even though a picture of a final judgement, with an eternal reward for those who enjoy divine favour, is found in a variety of religious traditions, these stories come with some philosophical puzzles when we see these outcomes as planned out by a very good and very powerful deity. These puzzles are distinct from any puzzles produced by trying to solve the traditional problem of evil discussed in Section 2. This section will examine what Zoroastrianism has to say about what will happen to people on the day of the final triumph of good over evil, and will discuss how an unexpected approach to this final sorting can offer new solutions to traditional puzzles about heaven and who is admitted to it.

The novel option suggested by combining some Zoroastrian texts about the 'final judgement' is that the purification people go through when evil is destroyed in the world leaves some people entirely intact, but results in some cases intermediate between surviving the process and being destroyed by it. There may be an option to say people are saved to a degree, and that there are cases where it is indeterminate whether someone made it to eternal bliss. Some Zoroastrian texts have some 'universalist' themes, suggesting that everyone is saved, and others suggest the evil are destroyed. Combining these apparently incompatible suggestions yields a 'quasi-universalism', according to which everyone makes it to heaven to some degree, but the worst of the evil-doers might share in heaven to a much lower degree than the righteous.

One reason this suggestion is of contemporary *philosophical* interest is that it offers distinctive responses to some puzzles in the philosophy of religion in making sense of a heavenly reward. After discussing some of these puzzles, and what the relevant Zoroastrian texts have to say, I will lay out how I think quasi-universalism can offer appealing responses to the problems, before turning to potential drawbacks of this approach. I will conclude the section with some reflections on quasi-universalism as an option for other faith traditions that endorse a heavenly afterlife for those favoured by the divine, especially Christian, Judaic, and Islamic traditions.

3.1 Puzzles about Salvation

The picture of a sorting into those admitted to heaven and those sent to hell, or even those admitted to heaven and those who undergo genuine destruction, has at least three things that are philosophically puzzling about it. The first is that alike cases seem to be treated very differently by most plans of salvation. One person is admitted to heaven while another, only slightly less worthy, is deprived of heaven altogether. Justice seems to require treating like cases alike, or at least not treating like cases in a radically different way. But the difference between salvation and not looks vast: perhaps infinitely separated in value. How could it be just to treat people who are not very far apart in worthiness in this infinitely different way?

Another issue that comes up with treating like people alike concerns differences between those admitted to heaven. Some are as good as human beings ever get and have done as well as anyone can do with respect to the things that merit heaven. Others have barely made it: had they been much worse in this life, they may not have made it to heaven in the next. Are those two groups of people granted the same level of reward? If so, then like cases have not been treated alike and some have not been treated with perfect justice. But if not, how could heaven be an ideal reward? On many conceptions of heaven an eternity in heaven is infinitely valuable, and perhaps even a day in heaven is infinitely valuable. Where is there room for treating unlike cases unalike when they are all experiencing an infinite reward?

The second set of issues is related to the first. Consider a range of very similar cases around the borderline of those to be saved. Given enough people with enough variation in what they have done in life, there is plausibly *vagueness* in whether some people are better than others, or have done more good than others, or have better performed their duties, or have done more good relative to their opportunities, or whatever it is that confers merit. This is true in the grey area as well. Plausibly, if some go to heaven and some do not, given a group of the 'least worthy' saved (call that group S), there will be people outside S about whom it is indeterminate whether they are at least as worthy as the members of S. For example, Barry is saved and Larry is not, but it is indeterminate whether Larry is as worthy as Barry. That looks unfair to Larry, or at best indeterminate whether it is fair. If a scheme of salvation is the best, it should not turn out that it is even indeterminate whether it is fair: we should expect it to be determinately fair. (This is a version of the problem of vagueness discussed by Sider 2002.)

The third is the question of why a very good, very powerful being would fail to save anyone: that is, why anyone is sent to hell or obliterated. The worst person did only a finite amount of harm and suffered from the limits that finite beings suffer from. Denying that person an infinite amount of good, as repayment for a finite amount of harm, looks disproportionate. Still worse if someone spends an eternity in hell as punishment for a finite amount of sin or defect in character: it looks like an all-good being would be more proportionate if she had the opportunity. (See a forceful discussion of the case that infinite suffering in hell would be a monstrous evil in Lewis 2007.) As mentioned in Section 2, another concern is similar to that articulated by Adams 1989. There are horrendous evils in the world, ones that it might surprise us that an all-good, all-powerful deity would allow. We might be tempted to think that an infinite reward in heaven 'makes up for' the unmerited evils some of us suffer in this life. But that seems to only make up for the evils suffered by people who eventually go to heaven. Suppose some people suffer horrendous evils, and then are thrown in hell or annihilated. The fact that some *other* people get a very nice afterlife does not seem to do much to justify the treatment of the victims who do not make it to heaven. I call this the *distributive* problem of evil: on the face of it, whatever makes up for evil or suffering should be outweighed by good *for the person enduring the evil and suffering*, and a divine plan where some suffer torment or even hell so that there is a good outcome that benefits other people is less than ideal, even if there is a high balance of good over evil overall.

One response to this third puzzle has been *universalism*: the doctrine that everyone will receive eternal life and go to heaven. That avoids having to answer the challenge of explaining why anyone goes to hell, through denying that anyone does. Adams 1989, pp. 306–307 suggests universalism as a response to what I called the distributive problem of evil: each person has the evil that has been done to them hugely outweighed by their eventual eternity in heaven. Universalism would resolve the first two problems raised above as well: like cases are all treated alike if everyone goes to heaven, and there are no cases where it is indeterminate that someone missed out on heaven who should have been sent there. (It does not do well in dealing with the challenge that it is unjust to treat unlike cases alike: those who achieve morally great things at great personal cost apparently get the same reward as the most vicious torturer.)

A final thought defended by some universalists is that anything less than universal salvation would represent a limitation on the success or triumph of God and redemption. As we saw in Section 2, Zoroastrians may be more willing to accept limits on the power of Ahura Mazda than some other faiths' attitudes to their gods, but even if Ahura Mazda is limited by Angra Mainyu during their struggle, it is natural to think that any limits Ahura Mazda faces now will be wiped out by his victory. Whether a failure to save everyone does represent a limitation depends on one's background view of what a deity is trying to achieve: if Ahura Mazda wishes to *defeat* those who firmly side with evil, denying them an infinite reward looks like a reasonable part of achieving that goal. If, on the other hand, he seeks only to defeat *evil*, rescuing even evil-doers from the clutches of Angra Mainyu looks like something he might prefer. As we will see, different parts of the Zoroastrian tradition line up with each of these outcomes. The option I will sketch here, however, is a surprising midway point between these two approaches.

Universalism about who will end up in heaven has able philosophical defenders, and many find it theologically satisfying as well. It has traditionally faced a number of objections. Some are theological ones: many religious traditions that talk of heaven also talk of hell, and it is hard to read either the Tanakh or the Bible or the Koran as implying that everyone goes to heaven. For that matter, it is hard to read, for example, Y32.6, 32.7 in the Gathas as suggesting that everyone goes to heaven. (Y32.15 in the Gathas also seems to contain a promise by Ahura Mazda to keep some people out of heaven, though as with any passage in the Gathas it is subject to contested interpretations.) Others are less tied to deciphering the contents of putative revelation, and concern questions about what would be morally ideal for a scheme of salvation. Some hold that universal salvation would be unjust, rewarding the most wicked in the same way as the morally best. Some hold that it undermines the requirement that we freely choose God over alternatives: you could argue that even omnipotence could not guarantee that everyone *freely* chooses to be with God. (Patsalidou 2012 is a useful introduction to some of the arguments about universalism in contemporary Christian theology.)

There is a strand of Zoroastrianism that is universalist, and holds that all human beings will have eternal blissful life after the defeat of evil. Another strand suggests the ultimate destruction of wicked human beings. I will argue in this section that there is a third option suggested by the combination Zoroastrian texts: that a sort of *quasi-universalism* might be implemented, giving us a sense in which everyone shares in the eternal reward and another sense in which not everyone makes it to the eternal blissful afterlife. The good will be admitted into heaven, but it is a matter of degree how much others are. This surprising option would give us distinctive responses to the problem of a dichotomy between heaven and no-heaven, the problem of vagueness and salvation, and an option with some of the advantages of universalism without some of the drawbacks.

In this section, I will focus on the distinction in salvation between going to heaven, on the one hand, and not going to heaven, on the other. Different stories of the afterlife differ about what happens to the people who do not end up in heaven. Two 'popular' options are first, that the unrighteous have an eternal afterlife filled with unpleasantness, whether that is the misery and torture of a hell or a gloomy mildly negative existence that seems to be the fate of most souls in Homer. The second option is that those not eventually admitted into heaven are destroyed and cease to exist entirely. Both of these outcomes strike me as infinitely less good for those who suffer them than heaven would be, which already generates the puzzles around the differences between those bound for heaven and those not. I am also going to largely neglect different accounts of what happens to us between now and the day of judgement. In traditions with a final day of reckoning, some hold that there is an afterlife of heaven or hell between death and *before* the final day. Various Zoroastrian texts have a lot of say about what happens in heaven and hell *between* death and the grand finale of the frasokereti, and elaborate on the stages of this process: see Shaked 1998, especially on 'universal eschatology'. While these states before the final judgement are also interesting from a theological and philosophical point of view, it would be distracting from my main topic to discuss them in any detail.

3.2 The Molten River

Near the end of the great conflict between Ahura Mazda and Angra Mainyu, evil will be burnt away by a great river of metal. The great flow of molten metal may be first mentioned in the Gathas, where the punishment of the evil is 'through the pure metal' (Ys 32.7, Kanga p 70). It receives a lot more elaboration in the *Bundahishn*, especially the so-called *Iranian Bundahishn*, compiled in the late ninth century CE.

The final triumph of good over evil (the *frasokereti*) will be triggered by a final saviour (Sayoshant) who will help Ahura Mazda vanquish evil once and for all, which will result in evil being entirely destroyed. As part of the destruction of evil in the world, all human beings who have died during the history of the world will undergo bodily resurrection, and then everyone will be made to walk through a river of molten metal. The good will find this a pleasant experience, akin to bathing in warm milk, while those who are less righteous will find their immersion in this molten metal a painful and unpleasant experience, during which the evil within them will be burned away (Greater Bundahishn 34: 19).

Our sources disagree about what happens to the truly wicked. The *Pahlavi Rivayat Accompanying the Dadestan i Denig* contains multiple accounts, probably because these are derived from distinct earlier traditions. In Pahlavi Rivayat 32.5, 36.4 (Williams 1983, pp. 425, 431), it says that the souls of the wicked will cease to exist. On the other hand, in Pahlavi Rivayat 48.70–72 (Williams 1983, pp. 461–462), even the most wicked human beings will be eventually purified and given eternal life. The perhaps more authoritative, and older, Greater Bundahishn (34.20) also takes this latter approach. 'Then all people will come together with great affection, fathers and sons, brothers and friends' (Agostini and Thrope 2020, p. 181).

This is not a complete account of Zoroastrian teachings about the afterlife and the frasokereti by any means, but it captures the important parts of the text we need to both raise the puzzles discussed earlier about people's ultimate afterlives, and provides the material to suggest a novel solution to some of the standard puzzles.

3.3 Modifying the Story

At this point, I will go beyond the sources, to point out an option the above story makes available. It is an option which gives this Zoroastrian eschatology distinctive resources to deal with the philosophical puzzles about the afterlife the paper began with. I have not found any evidence that our sources did develop the account in this way, though it does offer one way to do some justice to each of these apparently mutually inconsistent strands of Zoroastrian thought.

The river of molten metal 'refines' those who pass through it, removing any admixture of evil. Those who are already good and just suffer no discomfort, presumably because they have little or no evil to be burned out of them. Some of those who are less good and just suffer in the river as the evil within them is burned out, though they survive to emerge free of evil and ready for eternal life.

As previously mentioned, in some versions of the story reported above, the wicked are destroyed entirely, perhaps in the molten river, while in others everyone who enters the river emerges with their evil admixture destroyed and prepared for eternal heaven. One option I wish to explore is splitting the difference: that when even the most evil are purified *someone* emerges from the process, and that it may be a matter of degree, or not even determinate, whether the person who emerges is the person who begins the process. Of course the accounts of the river of metal, along with the rest of the prophecies of a final renovation of the world, may well not be taken literally, but I am assuming for the sake of this investigation they are at least intended to convey something significant about what a final triumph of good over evil would amount to.

Suppose that for each person, the purifying process results in a purely good person afterwards. (Perhaps some people are so good that the process leaves them unchanged, or perhaps everyone has some evil removed – a theological question to be resolved on another occasion.) The purification process *changes* those it purifies, in a significant way. The very good who are purified are changed very little, and the purified person at the end is determinately still them. It is possible to survive this process if one has a larger admixture of evil – but for those with a bit more evil, the change metaphorically (or literally!) burns away part of them, a change that is somehow bad for them while they go through it, even if it is morally uplifting.

What about the people who have as much evil in them as human beings can? On the model being proposed here, the evil is burned away and the person who steps out is perfectly good: but perhaps this change is so great that the person who steps out is no longer the person who steps in. Naturally, if some people determinately do not survive the process, it is plausible that there are people who indeterminately survive the process: a lot of what is important to them being the same person across time changes, but in the grey area between the people who definitely do make it and the people who definitely do not. (A more optimistic version of this story may hold that nobody determinately does not make it, while perhaps leaving room for indeterminacy about survival of the very worst people.)

Why would removing evil threaten the destruction of someone? We could offer answers about functional disruption or sheer amount of the earlier person disappearing, especially if we take the molten metal and the burning relatively literally. But those kinds of answers would suggest that the link between removing evil and destruction was only contingent, raising the question of why the evil was not removed in some more humane way. Better, perhaps, to look for an answer about why the amount of evil is *constitutively* relevant to whether a change is person-destroying. The general idea is that aspects of a person such as their character, dispositions to behave, attitudes to others and themselves, and so on are important to what makes that person the person they are. Change too many of those things too rapidly, and you have a numerically new person, and somewhere between definitely-a-new-person and definitely-the-same-earlier-person are indeterminate cases. Furthermore, this is not just a causal hypothesis about what sorts of changes people can survive: given the kinds of things people are, of metaphysical necessity, their continued existence requires not-too-radical-change of central facts about them as a person, at least over a quick transition.

This yields a position I will label 'quasi-universalism'. A version of each person goes to heaven, but the extent to which that version is the earlier person varies. For the fortunate blessed, it is determinate that the new version is numerically identical to them: determinately, the person who comes out of the river is the person who goes in. *Perhaps*, for some, it is determinate that their successor is *not* them: the purified morally perfect version of the most wicked might just be too different. Even in these cases, though, the person who emerges from the river is not entirely unlike the person who goes in: even in the worst-case scenario, someone who is a continuer of you will enter heaven. And in the indeterminate cases, it is indeterminate whether the person is saved. That is, their successor definitely enters heaven, but it is indeterminate whether the successor is the person who enters the molten river.

This option gives us distinctive answers to the problems of dichotomous outcomes, vagueness, and the distributive problem of evil. The extent to which one enters heaven appears to vary, so there is a continuum of outcomes to match the continuum of different states of character and goodness candidates have. When it is indeterminate whether someone should be saved, it can be indeterminate whether they are saved. And, arguably, even the wicked receive a portion of heaven, or something like it: even if, for example, someone who only counts as me to a 10% level is saved, that might be as good for me as 10% of salvation. Concerns that universalism treat the good and the wicked too much alike can also be assuaged: being near 100% in heaven beats being only 10% there. I will discuss further, in Section 3.4, whether these conclusions about this set-up can be sustained. But first let me turn to the topic of survival through radical change, to discuss whether it makes sense to think that there are processes of the right sort, that have a person in existence at the end that is not the person who began them, and how to understand possible processes we indeterminately survive.

3.4 Survival through Radical Change

One topic tackled by twentieth-century philosophers in the Anglo-American tradition was the question of personal identity over time. What did it take for people at different times to be one and the same person, and what were the limits to which processes someone could survive and which processes would result in their being no more? There are relatively clear cases on both sides of the divide. I can survive sitting down: I have done so many times, with the person in the chair being numerically identical to the person who was standing moments before. I cannot survive at the centre of a large bomb explosion: while investigators may be able to find some pieces that were part of my body, and while my friends will retain fond memories and ideally some of my writing will still be read, I would not literally live through being blown to smithereens. (Bracket, for now, the question of whether there might be some immortal soul that detaches from the body and continues, somehow, to be me.)

Slightly more interestingly, there are thought-experiment cases where there is a person after the process, who in some sense is a salient candidate to be the person at the start of the process, but we might not want to say the person afterwards is numerically the same person as the one before. Perhaps a science-fictional total brain-wipe and reset, that leaves a person in my body with the psychology of a new-born, is a process that I do not survive, but one where I am replaced with a new person in my body. Perhaps a case where both of my brain hemispheres are removed and placed in different artificial bodies is one where there are two new people, neither of whom is the person who is strapped to the operating table. (After all, each of the one-hemisphere people is numerically distinct from each other, so if they are both identical to the pre-operation person, they would each be identical to someone they are numerically distinct from. That looks impossible.)

There are not just science fiction cases to consider. Advanced dementia can leave a patient with few links to earlier memories or personality. Legally, these patients are treated as being the same person as the person in that body before dementia struck: care homes do not start a new medical record for them, and their age is recorded as if they have lived a long time, rather than that they are people who began late in the progress of dementia, and when they die wills that were composed before dementia set in may be enforced. But friends and relatives often talk as if the pre-dementia person is gone, and their body survives without their old friend there anymore. (Kindness and respect of various sorts is still due to the patient, but perhaps not because they are the same person who started to develop the condition.) There is an interesting philosophical question with practical import here about whether the same person is present throughout the illness in cases like this.

Cases that are less talked about are ones where a person's body, memories, and psychological capacities largely remain intact but they undergo large and rapid changes of character. Someone who changes overnight from being kind to being cruel, from being a humanitarian to being a sadistic serial killer, and who changes their outlook and evaluation of all of their projects, relationships and sensibilities, has undergone a large change in many of the aspects of personhood we care about. It would at least raise the question of whether we have the same person on our hands. (I have described the case as if one person has undergone this change, but we could describe it more neutrally so that we leave it open whether the Catherine who goes to sleep the night before is the Kate who wakes up with a very different character the next day.) We could make sense of Catherine's friends or family reacting as if Catherine is gone and Kate is a new person, perhaps one to be avoided or to warn people about. It seems to me a difficult question of whether the pre-change-person is numerically identical to the post-change-one, across a change this dramatic.

In the famous real-life case of Phineas Gage, Gage suffered serious brain damage as the result of an industrial accident, and his behaviour changed significantly as a result. While the truth might have been more prosaic, a popular legend grew up that Gage's behaviour and character changed dramatically as the result of his injury, to the extent that his personality became unrecognisable to his friends and family. Indeed, one of the doctors who treated him reported, in a famous passage, that Gage changed so radically that 'his friends and acquaintances said he was "no longer Gage"' (Harlow 1849, p. 17). Oliver Sacks reports a different case of a patient who underwent dramatic psychological shifts due to a brain tumour, to the point where the patient's father at one point described the patient as 'a sort of simulacrum or changeling' (Sacks 1995, p. 52). In both of these cases there were a lot of psychological continuities as well, and it is unclear whether this talk of no longer being the same person, or being a changeling, was intended as anything more than metaphorical. (In Sacks's case, there was plenty of other evidence that the patient's father treated the patient as being the same person as his pre-tumour son.) In some of the popular myth-making about Gage, various authors have talked about him becoming a new person after his accident. The public willingness to tell stories about Gage according to which a sufficient shift in personality and character make someone literally into a new person might itself show that our understanding of personal identity countenances that possibility: see

Rennick 2021 for a defence of the view that we can learn about our concepts through examining which fictions make sense to us.

Even less talked about is whether someone could survive a rapid *upgrade* of their character, projects, sensibilities, and so on. We might be relieved if a monstrous national leader were struck by 'moral lightning' and the person after the lightning strike had the same information and abilities but recoiled from injustice, did all they could to stop any cruelty they had unleashed, devoted their lives to good works, and so on. But it would raise the question of whether the post-strike person was numerically identical with the pre-strike one, even if they inhabited the same body, responded to the same name, and so on.

It could well be that there are large grey areas between the clear cases of person A and person B at different times being the same person, on the one hand, and being determinately distinct people, on the other. This seems to me especially plausible when we move away from real-life cases to thought-experiment cases. In the heat of the debate over personal identity in the twentieth century, philosophers often had clear intuitions about various outlandish cases, and notoriously different experts had clashing intuitions, but we might think that there are areas of vagueness and indeterminacy which we reach when we consider personality transplants, complex brain-splitting and rehousing, or hypothetical 'uploads' of people and multiple 'downloads' of different versions. Diagnosing indeterminacy in some of these cases might be particularly tempting when we realise that our judgements about cases can be sensitive to fairly fine-grained facts about how they are presented. Williams 1970 famously argued that whether we are inclined to think of a putative 'body swap' case as people switching bodies or people staying in their same bodies but with massive mental alterations can depend on the details of the presentation of the scenario. One natural reaction to Williams's discussion is to think that our concepts of persons and persons over time have less built into them than we might have originally supposed. (Williams 1970, pp. 177–178 also points out how difficult it would be, if we found ourselves in a scenario like his, to rest content with the thought that there was indeterminacy about whether we would move to a different body or not: whether that cuts against the idea that it *would* be indeterminate whether people switch bodies in the scenario, or just that we are not used to thinking our survival can be indeterminate, is a tricky question. I am inclined to think it more suggests the latter than the former.)

While it is natural to think that identity over time can be unusual in the ways described, having cases of indeterminacy and also being naturally described as coming in degrees, some contemporary philosophers will argue that this cannot be right. Identity always holds between a thing and itself to the highest degree possible, and holds between a thing and anything else to the lowest degree possible. Identity cannot be indeterminate either, some philosophers argue (e.g. Evans 1978 is often interpreted this way, though see Lewis 1988), which would preclude any indeterminate cases. Another worry lurking here is that the indeterminacy that comes with vagueness is only ever *epistemic*: that when we have indeterminate cases as a result of vagueness or otherwise, there *is* a sharp cutoff (e.g. between the people who survive and the people who do not), but the indeterminacy consists in our not knowing where that sharp dividing line is. (See Sorensen 1988, pp. 217–252 and Williamson 1994 for two influential defences of this epistemicism.) It would not do very well for providing intermediate cases between determinate survival and determinate non-survival if it was just that nobody *knew* whether some people were saved. (Even all-knowing Ahura Mazda?)

I am not as sceptical as some: I think talk of identity over time coming in degrees can be made good sense of, perhaps with some paraphrase, and I am willing to take appearances at face value and admit that there are cases where it is indeterminate whether a person at an earlier time is the same person as one at a later time. Furthermore, the epistemicist suggestion that whenever there is indeterminacy there is a hidden truth of the matter which is unknown or unknowable still seems implausible me, as it does to most philosophers thinking about vagueness and indeterminacy. Still, there are substantial commitments lurking here about identity over time and indeterminacy.

One available fall-back position would be to talk about *what matters* in survival coming in degrees, rather than survival itself coming in degrees. Parfit 1984 is one influential presentation of the idea that what we should care about when having self-directed concern towards someone at another time is not primarily whether that person is *ourselves*, but rather whether the person stands in a sufficiently rich set of relations to us at present: whether the person at another time is 'R-related' to us, and to what degree. Parfit thinks that, for example, in science-fictional teletransporter mishap cases, there might be several people who are near-copies of us running around, and we should be concerned about all of them to roughly the degree we are normally concerned about our future selves, even though Parfit does not think that each of those people in the future is *identical* to us now. They do have the psychological continuities of (quasi-)memory and other psychological processes that are the sorts of things that make for identity over time in more ordinary cases, which is what is needed for R-relatedness. (Parfit 1984, pp. 245–306). It would be anachronistic to interpret ancient Zoroastrians as Parfittians, but thinking about the relationship between pre-purification and post-purification people in terms of their degree of R-relatedness to each other is an option for those trying to make contemporary sense of quasi-universalism, but who do not think survival could literally come in degrees or be indeterminate.

Another part of the Zoroastrian story is that people who have a lot of evil burned out of them find this a painful and unpleasant process. Perhaps some of the originators of this story intended it literally, and it is reasonable that having parts burned out of one by molten metal would be painful. But can we make sense of this in more abstract terms? A greater challenge is to answer the question of why perfection of someone who begins as flawed or even somewhat evil would *best be carried out* through a painful and unpleasant process. If there is a merely causal explanation of the suffering, surely an all-good god of sufficient power could short-circuit the process and perfect someone without burning and agony?

I do not see any reason why damage must automatically be painful, but I think there is a case to be made that undergoing a radical change in one's character and certain crucial behavioural dispositions can be damaging. It disrupts one's values, aims, and projects, and enough of it can result in the destruction of the person we began with, at least if we share the intuition that sufficiently rewiring my brain might result in a new person altogether inhabiting my body, or no person left at all. It is no mere causal generalisation that if my desires, attitudes behavioural dispositions, and so on are rapidly changed by an outside force, then I have lost things of genuine value to me: aspects of my character, commitments, and take on the world just *are* valuable to me, and stripping those away is not *correlated* with losing something valuable, but *is* losing something of value to me. Perhaps these aspects of each of us are valuable to each of us: being evaluatively caught up in how one's own self is does not look as optional as, say, valuing sporting prowess, or valuing mountain ranges over grassy plains.

The idea that an evil person could be harmed just by being made less evil is not uncontroversial. There is of course a sense in which they are being *improved* by being made more morally excellent, which might seem to cut against the idea that they are harmed rather than helped. It might be useful to draw a distinction between something being morally improving for someone and something being self-interestedly or prudentially good for that person. There should be space for the thought that there are things that someone values about themselves that are not morally excellent about them, or even morally negative. Someone might value about themselves their biting wit or implacable thirst for vengeance, even if they would be morally better people if they lacked those things. Perhaps the idea is that truly evil people do value their traits, or even value *being those very people*, and being roughly the sort of way they are. Having that stripped away may be a negative thing for those people, given what they want, even if it is morally improving, perhaps even if, were they good and virtuous people they *would* value the removal of those evil aspects.

Perhaps an example would help. Take Alexander, the stock villain of so much Zoroastrian writing. (This is Alexander the Great – exalted by the Greeks as a conquering hero who extended Hellenistic domination across so much of the known world, but excoriated by the Persians as a destroyer who looted and dismantled so many temples to Ahura Mazda, destroyed the godly rule of the Achaemenid dynasty, killed and looted his way through so many lands, etc.) At least as the literary figure in Zoroastrianism, and perhaps in real life, Alexander is proud (treating himself as the son of a god), violent, enjoys war and conquest, fondly remembers with pride so much of the killing and destruction he caused, is disposed to enslave those who fall into his power, with a particular fondness for humiliation and sexual subjugation of noble Persian women, and so on. Alexander facing purification will lose all of that. Instead of being the lordly king and conqueror, he will be a kind and gentle person who wants to spend his time living peaceably and co-operatively with his fellows and communing with the god of the Persians, while regarding with horror so much of his old life. Even if, perhaps *per impossible*, Alexander is confident that he will survive the purification process, he may regard the process as removing many of the things that are valuable to him, and he may be right to see himself as being thereby harmed.

3.5 Problems Solved by This Approach

As previously discussed, three philosophical puzzles about the moral coherence of accounts of a final judgement stand out in particular. One concerns arbitrariness, with the thought that sufficiently dichotomous rewards and punishments do not treat like cases alike, and in particular it is puzzling how it could be just that one person receives infinite rewards while someone almost as deserving gets nothing, or worse. A second is a puzzle about vagueness: when it is indeterminate what someone's reward should be, how does a determinate infinite reward or a determinate lack of it answer to the case? Finally, there is the problem of why an omnibenevolent being who has the power to save everyone would leave anyone behind. This is particularly puzzling if those not sent to heaven are tortured forever, but even dividing everyone into the people who are saved and the people to be annihilated also seems like a less than omnibenevolent outcome. Let us look at what quasi-universalism can offer in the context of each of these puzzles.

What is distinctive about quasi-universalism that plays a role in addressing all of these puzzles is that there is a salvation that *comes in degrees*. The righteous who are barely affected by purification and those who become entirely good without impinging on their continued survival are saved and have the best outcome. Those who undergo so much change in the purification process that it is not entirely determinate whether the post-purification person is the same as the person before purification, and in extreme cases, it is determinate that a new person emerges from the process, albeit one who retains important continuities with the pre-purification individual. This helps only if we adopt an understanding of infinite reward so that having it to a less-than-maximal-degree is less valuable, all in all, than having it to a higher degree. The simplest way to represent infinite value swamps distinctions we might want to mark: if we were to set the value of heaven at aleph-nought, the 'countable infinity' of standard transfinite set theory, then adding any finite amount, subtracting any finite amount, or even multiplying it by a finite non-zero amount would leave it unchanged. But that does not preclude employing more complicated representations of infinite value that preserve many of the comparisons between infinitely valuable options we want. (For a much richer formal theory of value that might do the trick, see Chen and Rubio 2020.)

The problem of arbitrariness suggests that justice requires a graded series of rewards and punishments. Quasi-universalism offers that for people across a wide range of cases: while in every case your perfected version will be in heaven, if that perfected version is only 80% you this is less of a reward than for those for whom it will be 90% them, and more than those who survive only to a 60% or 50% degree. It is true that the tradition teaches that the truly righteous will all survive the river, and so the purification they encounter may not match their comparative merits exactly: several people might survive to 100% even though some are greater heroes than others. But it does not seem unjust to distribute 100% of an infinite reward to many of the worthy and righteous, especially if, as discussed in Section 2, infinite rewards might be distinguished in other ways, so that some heroes have a better eternity than others (e.g. a more merited one), even if all have an excellent and infinitely valuable one. If nobody is 0% continuous with their perfected version, then plausibly everyone receives some reward for the good aspects of their lives. It is rare, or perhaps it never happens, that a human being has nothing morally good about them and never has any good thoughts, good words, or good deeds.

Secondly, there are problems of *vagueness* (Sider 2002). As previously mentioned, there are two problems. The first is that, given a spectrum from the most deserving to the least, it is plausible that there is a grey area between those who merit admission to heaven and those who do not. But on more usual schemes of salvation, heaven is up-or-out: either someone eventually makes it to eternal bliss or they do not, with no (permanent) middle ground. Related to this first problem, it can often be indeterminate who has a morally better track record and character (or whatever it is that goes into an assessment of reward-worthiness). If A goes to heaven but B does not, it should not be indeterminate whether B was more worthy of salvation than A.

Quasi-universalism looks like it can match both kinds of vagueness. The first may be matched perfectly. Between those who determinately survive the river and those (if any) who determinately do not, there may well be cases of people about who it is *indeterminate* whether the person who steps out of the molten river is the person who stepped in: the person who stepped out is quite different in identity-determining respects, but not so different as to definitely be a new person. For people in this situation facing the river, it is indeterminate whether they should reach heaven *and* indeterminate whether they will.

As for the second problem, it may be that the indeterminacy of survival is multi-faceted and itself subject to higher-order vagueness. I have been talking as if we can boil the degree of survival down to something that can be represented by a single number (80% survival vs 100%, for example). But this is likely a simplification: at any rate I do not have any worthiness-meter at hand to examine to compare to a survival-meter suspended over the great river of metal. It may well be that in some cases it is indeterminate whether A or B is more survival-worthy, and *also* indeterminate which of A or B survived to a greater degree.

The third problem is whether a scheme of the eventual fates of everyone in the afterlife is one that an all-good deity could operate, compatible with their maximal goodness. As I discussed in Section 2, it is natural to interpret Zoroastrianism as denying Ahura Mazda's omnipotence: much of the evil in the world today are things Ahura Mazda would prevent if he could, but the battle with Angra Mainyu is a genuine contest and good has not triumphed yet. But after the triumph of good over evil Ahura Mazda is meant to have a much freer hand. What he does with everyone at that point does not seem limited, suggesting that whatever final scheme he implements should reflect his maximal goodness.

Leaving anyone out of granting infinite value to people would already be puzzling: why not ensure more value rather than less? Leaving anyone out might be puzzling even if we do not think they, or anyone, *deserve* heaven or have some claim to it. But an omnibenevolent being acts with mercy and compassion as well (or the divine equivalents), and it is natural to think such a being would save whoever they can, unless faced with an important reason not to. It would be particularly puzzling that some were left unsaved if an omnibenevolent being had an additional reason to bestow eternal bliss on each of us. Adams 1989 suggests one such reason. She argues that omnibenevolent beings would not want there to be uncompensated 'horrendous evils': evils or suffering so great that they cast into doubt whether a life that contains them would be 'a great good'. We can go further: even if an evil does not threaten to make the overall value of a life less than good, there are bad things that happen to people that an omnibenevolent being would rather we not undergo, and failing that would want our lives to be good enough elsewhere to swamp the disvalue of those evils. *One* way an omnipotent, omnibenevolent being could make up for such evils is to ensure that those who suffer them also have lives of infinite value. A few years of pain and sorrow followed by an eternity of heaven would be overall worth it.

We might of course doubt that Adams solves the problem of why a Christian deity might allow horrendous evils to be inflicted. Maybe an awful mortal coil followed by heaven would be overall a very positive good, but it seems to still be significantly less good than an unblighted mortal life followed by eternal heavenly bliss. But another aspect of Adams's response to horrendous evil may give us another (*pro tanto*) reason to adopt universalism conditional on Christian commitments. This is the *distributive* problem of evil: allowing for a scheme where some suffer great harm calls for a swamping of those harms *for the person who suffers them*, and not just a compensating valuable feature in the world as a whole. If a deity allows for me to be tortured when it could be avoided, it is not enough if someone somewhere gets something of great value. For example, it would not be enough that the torturers get to enjoy valuable autonomy, or the aesthetic features of a variegated world including some tastefully arranged episodes of torture are particularly prizeworthy.

Even though Adams concentrates on 'horrendous evils', one way to ensure nobody is left net-worse-off by the finite evils of our world is to give everyone an afterlife of infinite positive value. Otherwise, there is the risk that someone suffers great evils in this life and then undergoes damnation or oblivion, and there is the risk that *they* have not been treated as an omnibenevolent being would wish, no matter how much other value there is in the world. Arguably, there is some reason an omnibenevolent being would wish to massively outweigh the evil any victim of evil has endured.

No doubt it remains controversial that an omnibenevolent being would confer an infinitely valuable afterlife on all human beings if she could. Quasi-universalism does not quite say this, but it has many of the theoretical benefits of universalism while tempering some of the drawbacks.

If we all *to some extent* participate in an infinite reward, the reward all of us face might be enough to outweigh the harms or evils we have endured. Even if Alexander only 5% survives into a heavenly afterlife, the value of that might still be greater than any finite value. On the other hand, there is some dependence of reward on moral status, since a Zoroastrian saint who 100% survives receives a greater reward than the one received by the five percenter. This parries the objection that it is unjust that the worst villain receive the same reward as the most virtuous, without needing differences in heavenly experience for those who are there. This also means that the size of the reward can reflect the free moral choices of people in this life, responding to a concern that some anti-universalists have about universalism not reflecting the sort of dependence of our afterlife on our actions they think is required.

Finally, quasi-universalism enables the afterlife to be a motivation more than universalism seems to. If you are going to receive the same infinite bliss as the saints whatever you do, staying on the straight and narrow to get to heaven seems pointless. But if there is a difference between 100% coming through the purification process or only 80%, or even 80% rather than 60%, that seems to be a reason to prefer to be better than worse. (And the prospect itself of being perfected might lead one to hope to be in good moral shape before the process – it does not sound good in prospect to have one's personality and character disrupted, if that can be avoided.) I am not sure myself that a religion should encourage people to do the right thing for pie in the sky when they die, as opposed to the intrinsic value of right action and good outcomes, but anti-universalists do sometimes object to universalism for damaging the motivation that the prospect of heaven might otherwise provide.

3.6 Drawbacks of This Account

The account of the final judgement as one where everyone undergoes purification, and the post-purification people are sometimes clearly the ones who started the process but sometimes are not clearly the same people, can be deployed to give interesting answers to a raft of problems that have been raised for accounts of heaven, hell, and a final judgement. But some will have theological or philosophical concerns about this picture, and it is worth sketching what some of those might be.

One is of course epistemological: what reason do any of us have, Zoroastrians or non-Zoroastrians, to believe this account? Zoroastrians may wish to adopt doctrines about divine revelation as a source of knowledge, and then look at what theory best fits the authoritative sources. Here I think quasi-universalism is in the spirit of a range of Zoroastrian texts, but I do not say it follows from them. I am more interested in the view as a philosophically interesting and distinctive one that is Zoroastrian in spirit, though some Zoroastrians may wish to go further and believe it on the basis of what best makes sense of the strands of their traditions.

Those who do not recognise Zarathustra as a religious authority, or have faith in the tradition he founded, may well have less reason to accept this account. While the Section 3.7 will discuss some parallels to this eschatology in some Christian and Jewish traditions, my guess is that the appeal, if any, of this sort of story for contemporary theists will be on philosophical grounds. Puzzles about salvation suggest a good plan for admission to heaven might come in degrees and handle indeterminate cases indeterminately, for example.

Another concern comes from its resemblance to theological universalism. Some have thought that considerations of justice preclude everyone, no matter how much harm they do or how evil they are, from receiving an eternal, infinite reward. The view sketched above suggests that at least a version of everyone, no matter how vile they are, gets eternal bliss, and it plausibly entails that everyone *to some degree* receives eternal salvation. One might think that justice requires that some of the worst torturers and abusers do not receive even some degree of infinite happiness as their reward. True, the evil and wicked do suffer whatever harm purification inflicts, but that can seem disproportionately small when stacked against the evil some human beings do. This concern could be alleviated somewhat if we think that some evil people completely and determinately do not survive the purification process: 0% of a reward might seem about the right amount for some of the worst people to have lived. But just as there is a strong sentiment in some quarters against traditional universalism about salvation, there will likely be a strong sentiment against quasi-universalism.

On the other hand, pro-universalists might take the account I have sketched above to not go far enough. Universalists often think anything less than salvation of all would be a less than optimal outcome: a blemish on omnipotence, omnibenevolence, or both. Zoroastrian universalists might concede that the quasi-universalism I have sketched would not be terrible, but perhaps an even greater victory over evil would be achieved by determinately, 100%, saving everyone? (Or all humanity – maybe Angra Mainyu/Ahriman and his daiwas can be destroyed, according to taste.) While I have sketched reasons why we might think that, of metaphysical necessity, some evil people cannot be perfected by a one-step or few-step procedure, I would not blame Zoroastrians who thought, on theological grounds, that Ahura Mazda will somehow get around these apparent limitations and render his victory complete in a way fully satisfying to a universalist.[2]

---

[2] Some Parsi Zoroastrians have adopted a doctrine of transmigration or reincarnation, where some or all human souls reappear in new human bodies, perhaps again and again until the end of struggle. (See Kreyenbroek and Munshi, pp. 149, 226 and reference in their index.) While some other Zoroastrians consider this unorthodox, it could give universalists extra resources: even if a person seems essentially less than good in one life, they have time and experience enough to change in subsequent lives. Alexander the Great is a stock evil figure in traditional Zoroastrian literature, but perhaps subsequent lives of kindness and service would qualify even him to walk through molten metal unharmed. CZC 2024, while saying that not all Zoroastrians accept reincarnation, is explicit that this reincarnation is so that people can become perfected across multiple lives.

Yet another concern is about whether it is the *best* way to ensure an eternal heavenly life. (And if it is not, whether it could be the design of a deity who is supposed to be omnibenevolent.) I have suggested that, given how some people are at the end of their lives, transforming them into someone perfect and free from evil would compromise their identity in a way that would be damaging and somehow negative for them. Why not perfect someone in a way that is not damaging or negative? There are two options here. One is to give people unsuited for heaven in their current state their own kind of infinitely valuable afterlife that does not require reform: perhaps an endless exciting video game or a Valhalla of fighting and drinking. The other would be to perfect people in a painless and undamaging way.

This first option is potentially unsatisfactory in a number of ways. Perhaps those other afterlives are too much less valuable than heaven, so that it would be even better to perfect them and give them an afterlife suitable for the morally perfect than an eternity of something more mundane. Or perhaps there is something morally suspect about leaving the wicked unregenerated. Or perhaps the good of transforming the world into an evil-free-zone requires the purification of evildoers. A second option is to perfect someone without inflicting any damage or suffering. This seems initially more appealing, but I think the best thing for a quasi-universalist to say is that not even omnipotence could perfect some evildoers without this kind of disruption: the metaphysically essential facts, or the essence of personhood, or something similar rules out a non-disruptive externally imposed perfecting of some people. (There is of course the question of why permit there to be evil people in the first place, a problem of evil I will not tackle here.)

A final concern is raised by the talk of the righteous meriting salvation in the first place. One approach to salvation, particularly associated with Martin Luther is that nobody deserves salvation, and nothing we can do can merit salvation more than anything else: it is an unconstrained application of God's grace, which nobody can merit. Presumably, on this view, it would be no stain on perfect goodness to not save even the best, most kind, and most loving among us.

It is open, of course, to Zoroastrians to reject this picture of salvation, and to think an omnibenevolent deity like Ahura Mazda *would* appropriately respond to the merit of the righteous by ensuring they have eternal life, and it would be less good of him not to. But even those attracted to the view that no human being has a claim on eternal bliss can think that it would be a *good thing* for a deity to reward the good or save the middling from oblivion or damnation. Even if it is a gift that Ahura Mazda was not morally obligated to bestow, a plan of rewarding the good, and perhaps rewarding the less good in a lesser way, does not need the recipients to *deserve* the reward in some strong sense to be something an all-good deity would arrange.

3.7 What about Other Theists?

Whether or not the picture sketched is a satisfying response to the problems about eternal reward on its own terms, it has some features that may make it less appealing to theists from other traditions. Some are metaphysical: not everyone believes that we are mixtures of good and evil, at least not in any way that a picture of refining out the good from the evil would make sense. Other problems are more epistemic: the authorities recognised by a typical Christian or Muslim, for example, do not include Zoroastrian religious authorities, so theists in those traditions may feel they have little reason to endorse anything like the picture presented above.

It is no part of the goal of this section to tell anyone, including Zoroastrians, what they should believe about a final judgement or a beatified state or eternal life. But it might be interesting to some to see how the kind of strategy sketched above might appeal to some believers in an afterlife who do not share the specific religious and metaphysical commitments that have been outlined.

The idea that God might have in heaven purified and perfected versions of ourselves is common in many traditions besides Zoroastrianism: Christian heaven is supposed to be a place without sin, without pain, without fear, in which we have eternal life, for example. The story that souls are purified in molten metal before entry to heaven may be familiar to some readers, since a very similar metaphor appears early in the Christian tradition. Clement of Alexandria, his student Origen, and later Gregory of Nyssa all talk of an *apocatastasis*, or restoration of the world to a sinless perfection, and all talk of the need for some people to be purified or refined by divine fire. Origen at least appears to adopt a universalist take on this story, according to which every soul is eventually purified and joins God in heaven. (It is more controversial how to interpret the passages of Gregory that suggest universal salvation through purification by fire.) See Sachs 1993 for a discussion of all three.

Clement, Origen and Gregory claim to find New Testament support for the idea that wrongdoers will be purified by a refining fire, and that the fire and brimstone of hell serve a purifying function, at least in part. While passages such as Mark 9:43 and 9:49 are cited, the main passages that seem to prompt this refining reading are Revelations 19-21. The 'restoration of all things' by God at some future time is suggested by passages such as Matthew 17:11 and especially Acts 3:19-21 also appear to have suggested to Clement and Origen that there would be a process that could appropriately be described, metaphorically at least, with the metaphor of refining fire.

The image of God refining the good with fire and destroying the evil is also present in the pre-Christian Jewish tradition, which likely explains its presence in Christian thought. In the book of Malachi, the last book of the *Tanakh*, God tells his prophet that 'He will come to judge like one who refines and purifies silver', purifying the priests in particular (3:3), and later that 'the day is coming when all proud and evil people will burn like straw. They will burn up, and there will be nothing left of them' (4:1). At least in Malachi, this refining fire destroys those sufficiently wicked: it is unclear whether anyone entirely escapes the purification process, though presumably some need more purification than others and those judged more harshly suffer more.

It might well be that the Judaic and then Christian traditions borrow these ideas and imagery from Zoroastrianism (see e.g. Boyce and Grenet 1991, p. 367), and it is possible that it is the other way around, though my impression is that scholars of Zoroastrianism rarely attribute much of Zoroastrian doctrine to Judaism or Christianity. Texts like the Iranian Bundahishn are undoubtedly compiled much later than early Christian texts such as those of Clement or Gregory, but *may* represent traditions going back to the time of Zarathustra, or to any time in between that and the date of compilation. So it is hard to be sure why similar ideas turn up in these interacting traditions.

Reflection on the story of the molten river might also help in thinking specifically about the Roman Catholic doctrine of purgatory. The Catholic doctrine of purgatory is that those who are 'imperfectly purified' but not excluded from heaven undergo a post-death period of 'purification' in a state called purgatory. It is often described as involving the purifying burning of those in purgatory, though perhaps this is intended less literally than in the Avesta and Bundahishn. (For a recent example, then-pope Benedict XVI described it as 'transforming burning' in 2007 in the encyclical *Spe Salvi* (Benedict 2007).)

One traditional puzzle about purgatory is why God would not, or could not, just forgive sins and allow the person into heaven straight away. If the person is bound for eternal life and happiness in any case, suffering in the fires of purgatory first looks like a gratuitous infliction of suffering. Even if those in hell are irredeemable in some way, presumably this is not true of the inhabitants of purgatory. Various answers could be offered here: perhaps purgatory is the only way to guarantee the appropriate kind of repentance needed as a precondition for heaven, or it is for the benefit of those still alive to give them a chance to do good works by interceding for those in purgatory, or justice demands the punishment of sin in a way that makes more mercy than that shown inappropriate.

The story sketched has another answer. Changing someone in respects crucial to whether the subsequent person even is the earlier person is disruptive. Even when it results in moral improvement, the process is bad for the person who undergoes it, in the ways suggested above, and may even be experienced as unpleasant. But since this improvement of character and moral dispositions is essential to this sort of personal transformation, God cannot just bring the person up to standard without the disruption. So purgatory, on this view, is not an optional step God has imposed in order to make the afterlife worse for those needing improvement, but a necessary accompaniment to perfecting them, to make the most of the eternity of heaven which awaits.

More abstractly, many who believe in a heavenly afterlife may be tempted by the idea that we undergo a transformation from our material lives to our heavenly selves, and that this transformation is disruptive for people with bad characters and dispositions. Many hold that heavenly selves would be without sin and perhaps without the disposition to sin: and this might require changes in character and outlook from most of us, and perhaps radical changes for some. If it is plausible that character, moral values and dispositions in morally weighty situations play an important role in what it is to be us, then those attracted by the hope of heaven may wish to think about how God can ensure those perfected beings really are the same people as our sinful selves.

The story of purification will not appeal to all religious traditions. For example, those who take the ideal end-state to be non-existence, or alternatively the lack of any desires or preferences or other conative states, will likely not find any notion of heaven as eternal life to be the sort of thing an all-good being would want for his creation. Some may think we are already fitted for heaven, and no purification or improvement is required, especially not any that is disruptive to who we currently are. As previously mentioned, there are those who think it is a mistake to tie going to heaven to any notion of merit, and they are unlikely to think the character of the saved needs to be sufficiently good. No doubt there are other ways to resist even the broad outline of the picture presented here. However, for traditions have wanted to make sense of infinite reward and punishment, salvation after death or the prospect of eternal life that is somehow better or preferable to the state we currently find ourselves in, quasi-universalism embraces many strands of such traditions while giving distinctive resolutions to the puzzles about heaven sketched at the start of this section.

One thing to keep in mind is that there are a range of attitudes to this suggestion that might make sense besides outright belief and outright disbelief. Some theists hesitate to believe *anything* too specific about an afterlife or a final judgement: they might, for example, be confident that God has a good and satisfying plan without opinions about what that is exactly. The option sketched here might be useful for them as a 'how possibly' option: it is one way to have many of the benefits of a story about admission to heaven without some of the standard drawbacks. Or perhaps a satisfying attitude towards accounts like this is *hope* that something like it is true, or 'looking for' something like it to be true. (When the Christian Nicene Creed says that its subscribers 'look for the resurrection of the dead', maybe it just means they believe the dead will be resurrected, but perhaps it is some optimistic state that does not necessarily involve belief.) Quasi-universalism has some pleasing features, so perhaps some theists not prepared to believe it may wish to take up less committal but positive attitude towards it.

3.8 Conclusion

A doctrine where every person being purified results in *a* person fit for heaven afterwards, but where it can be a matter of degree how much the person after the process is the same as the person who begins the process, helps to solve a number of puzzles about the moral satisfactoriness of the afterlife. This quasi-universalism admittedly goes beyond the texts we have about souls passing through the refining river of metal: while it is one way to give something to the tradition that everyone survives purification, on the one hand, and to the tradition that some definitely do and some definitely do not, on the other, I do not want to suggest it is the only way to make sense of this part of Zoroastrian eschatology. I have focused on it instead because it offers distinctive, and perhaps attractive, responses to problems that face traditions about a final judgement found across a range of religious traditions.

One question I have not addressed in this section is whether we *should* seek a satisfying story about heaven and hell. Some strands of some religious traditions have suggested that the divine plan should be inscrutable, and that we should expect the flashes of revelation we have collectively received should be hard to make sense of as a whole. While I do not intend to prescribe any understanding to Zoroastrians of their own faith, the impression I get from Zoroastrian religious texts, at least, is that the all-good Ahura Mazda does show an interest in making sense to his followers, and expects them to be informed participants in the great project of overcoming evil and promoting the eventual triumph of good. Ahura Mazda, at least, is not portrayed as capricious or unfathomable; rather, he wants us to share in his project. So I think it would be reasonable for Zoroastrians to hope that Ahura Mazda's overall plan can make good sense to them, and that their faith can be intellectually as well as spiritually satisfying.

References

Adams, M. M. (1989). Horrendous Evils and the Goodness of God. *Aristotelian Society Supplementary Volume*, 63(1), 297–323. https://doi.org/10.1093/aristoteliansupp/63.1.297.

Agostini, D. and Thrope, S. (2020). *The Bundahišn*. Oxford: Oxford University Press.

Anita, K. H. (2015). *The Argument for Acceptance in Zoroastrianism*. Monee, IL: CreateSpace Independent.

Anklesaria, B. T. (trans.) (1956). *Zand-Akasih–Iranian or Greater Bundahishn*. Bombay: Rahnumae Mazdayasnan Sabha.

Azadpur, M. (2007). Hegel and the Divinity of Light in Zoroastrianism and Islamic Phenomenology. *Classical Bulletin*, 82(2), 227–246.

Benedict XVI. (2007). Spe Salvi. *The Holy See,* https://www.vatican.va/content/benedict-xvi/en/encyclicals/documents/hf_ben-xvi_enc_20071130_spe-salvi.html (Accessed 28 March 2024).

Boyce, M. (1975). *A History of Zoroastrianism, Volume 1, Early Period*. Leiden: Brill.

(1982). *A History of Zoroastrianism, Volume 2, Under the Achaemenians*. Leiden: Brill.

(1997). The Origins of Zoroastrian Philosophy. In B. Carr and I. Mahalingam (eds.), *Companion Encyclopedia of Asian Philosophy*. London: Routledge, pp. 4–20.

Boyce, M. and Grenet, F. (1991). *A History of Zoroastrianism, Volume 3, Zoroastrianism under Macedonian and Roman Rule*. Leiden: Brill.

Boyd, J. W. and Crosby, D. A. (1979). Is Zoroastrianism Dualistic or Monotheistic?. *Journal of the American Academy of Religion*, 47(4), 557–588.

Cantera, A. (2015). Ethics. In M. Stausberg, Y. S. Vevaina, and A. Tessmann (eds.). *The Wiley-Blackwell Companion to Zoroastrianism*. London: Wiley-Blackwell, pp. 315–332.

Cereti C. G. (2014). Škand Gumānīg Wizār. In *Encyclopædia Iranica*, online edition, www.iranicaonline.org/articles/shkand-gumanig-wizar (Accessed 8 November 2024).

Chen, E. K. and Rubio, D. (2020). Surreal Decisions. *Philosophy and Phenomenological Research*, 100(1), 54–74. https://doi.org/10.1111/phpr.12510.

References

CZC (Californian Zoroastrian Center). (2024). About Zoroastrianism. www.czc.org/about-zoroastrian (Accessed 3 November 2024).

Darmesteter, J. and Mills, L. H. (1880–1887). *The Zend-Avesta (Parts I-III)*, Sacred Books of the East Volumes 4, 23, 31. Oxford: Clarendon. Online version, https://sacred-texts.com/sbe/index.htm.

Dhabhar, B. N. (trans.) (1932). *Persian Rivayats of Hormazyar Framarz and Others*. Bombay: K.R. Kama Oriental Institute, pp. 437–457. The two Ulema-i Islam texts translated by Dhabhar. www.avesta.org/mp/ulema.htm.

de Jong, A. (2014). Zurvanism. In *Encyclopedia Iranica*, online edition, www.iranicaonline.org/articles/zurvanism (Accessed 3 November 2024).

Evans, G. (1978). Can There Be Vague Objects? *Analysis*, 38, 208. https://doi.org/10.1093/analys/38.4.208.

Gignoux, P. (1994). Denkard. In *Encyclopedia Iranica*, online edition, www.iranicaonline.org/articles/denkard (Accessed 6 November 2024).

Harlow, J. M. (1849). *Recovery from the Passage of an Iron Bar Through the Head*. Boston: David Clapp and Sons.

Hassan, P. (2021). Nietzsche's Genealogical Critique and the Historical Zarathustra. *Ergo*, 7(24), 626–658. https://doi.org/10.3888/ergo.1121.

Hick, J. (1978). *Evil and the God of Love, Revised Edition*. San Francisco: Harper and Row.

Hintze, A. (2004). On the Ritual Significance of the Yasna Haptaŋhāiti. In M. Stausberg (ed.), *Zoroastrian Rituals in Context*. Leiden: Brill, pp. 291–306.

(2013). *Change and Continuity in the Zoroastrian Tradition*. London: SOAS, University of London.

Horky, P. S. (2009). Persian Cosmos and Greek Philosophy: Plato's Associates and the Zoroastrian *Magoi*, *Oxford Studies in Ancient Philosophy*, 37, 47–103.

Kanga, K. E. (1997). *Gāthā-Bā-Maāni* (trans. M. F. Kanga). Bombay: Trustees of the Parsi Panchayat Funds and Properties.

Kreyenbroake, P. G. and Munshi, S. N. (2001). *Living Zoroastrianism*. Richmond, Surrey: Curzon Press.

Kronen, J. D. and Menssen, S. (2010). The Defensibility of Zoroastrian Dualism. *Religious Studies*, 46(2), 185–205. https://doi.org/10.1017/s0034412509990357.

Lauwers, L. and Vallentyne, P. (2004). Infinite Utilitarianism: More Is Always Better. *Economics and Philosophy*, 20(2), 307–330. https://doi.org/10.1017/s0266267104000227.

Lewis, D. (1988). Vague Identity: Evans Misunderstood. *Analysis*, 48(3), 128–130. https://doi.org/10.1093/analys/48.3.128.

(1993). Evil for Freedom's Sake? *Philosophical Papers*, 48(2), 206–212. https://doi.org/10.1080/05568649309506401.

(2007). Divine Evil. In L. Anthony (ed.), *Philosophers Without Gods: Meditations on Atheism and the Secular Life*. New York: Oxford University Press, pp. 231–242.

Mackie, J. L. (1982). *The Miracle of Theism*. Oxford: Oxford University Press.

Maneck, S. S. (1997). *The Death of Ahriman: Culture, Identity and Theological Change Among the Parsis of India*. Bombay: K.R. Cama Oriental Institute.

Mardānfarrox. (2015). *The Doubt-Removing Book of Mardānfarrox*, trans. Raham Asha. Erman: Alain Mole.

Mariani, E. E. (2020). Nietzsche und die Worte des Avestā. Lektürespuren parsischer Texte in Also Sprach Zarathustra *Nietzsche Studien*, 49(1), 276–291. https://doi.org/10.1515/nietzstu-2020-0012.

Meisami, S. (2023). Light/Darkness Dualism and Islamic Metaphysics in Persianate Context. In M. Rustom (ed.), *Festschrift in Honor of William C. Chittick and Sachiko Murata*. Leiden: Brill, pp. 371–388.

Motameni, A. R. (2014). *Iranian Philosophy of Religion and the History of Political Thought*. UC Riverside Electronic Theses and Dissertations. https://escholarship.org/uc/item/8t2507mw (Accessed 5 November 2024).

Mulgan, T. (2002). Transcending the Infinite Utility Debate. *Australasian Journal of Philosophy*, 82, 164–177. https://doi.org/10.1093/ajp/80.2.164.

Narten, J. (1986). *Der Yasna Haptaŋhāiti*. Weisbaden: Reichert.

Nolan, D. (2023). Zurvanist Supersubstantivalism. *Asian Journal of Philosophy*, 2(38), 1–19. https://doi.org/10.1007/s44204-023-00090-2.

Otto, R. (2021). Zoroaster and the Animals. *Journal of Animal Ethics*, 11(2), 73–82. https://doi.org/10.5406/janimalethics.11.2.0073.

Patsalidou, I. (2012). Universalism and the Problem of Hell. *Philosophy Compass*, 7(11), 808–820. https://doi.org/10.1111/j.1747-9991.2012.00520.x.

Plantinga, A. (1974). *God, Freedom and Evil*. Grand Rapids: William B Eerdmans.

Parfit, D. (1984). *Reasons and Persons*. Oxford: Clarendon Press.

Rennick, S. (2021). Trope Analysis and Folk Intuitions. *Synthese*, 199(1–2), 5025–5043. https://doi.org/10.1007/s11229-020-03013-3.

Rose, J. (2011). *Zoroastrianism: An Introduction*. London: I.B. Tauris.

Rowe, W. (1979). The Problem of Evil and Some Varieties of Atheism. *American Philosophical Quarterly*, 16, 335–341.

Sachs, J. R. (1993). Apocatastasis in Patristic Theology. *Theological Studies*, 54(4), 615–788. https://doi.org/10.1177/004056399305400402.

Sacks, O. (1995). *An Anthropologist on Mars*. Sydney: Picador.

Sanjana, P. D. B. (ed.) (1876). *The Denkard* (trans. Rantanshah E. Kohiyar). Avesta.org, www.avesta.org/denkard/dk3s.html (Accessed 14 November 2024).

Shaked, S. (1992). The Myth of Zurvan Cosmology and Eschatology. In I. Gruenwald, S. Shaked, and G. G. Stroumsa (eds.), *Messiah and Christos: Studies in the Jewish Origins of Christianity: Presented to David Flusser on the Occasion of this Seventy-Fifth Birthday*. Tubingen: Mohr Siebeck, pp. 219–240.

(1998). Eschatology i: In Zoroastrianism and Zoroastrian Influence. In *Encyclopedia Iranica*, online edition, https://iranicaonline.org/articles/eschatology-i (Accessed 11 April 2024).

Sider, T. (2002). Hell and Vagueness. *Faith and Philosophy*, 19, 58–68. https://doi.org/10.5840/faithphil20021918.

Skjærvø, P. O. (2012). Kartir In *Encyclopædia Iranica*, online edition, www.iranicaonline.org/articles/kartir (Accessed on 6 November 2024).

Sorensen, R. (1988). *Blindspots*. Oxford: Oxford University Press.

Stewart, J. (2018). *Hegel's Interpretation of the Religions of the World: The Logic of the Gods*. Oxford: Oxford University Press.

Stausberg, M., Veviana, Y. S., and Tessman, A. (eds.) (2015). *The Wiley-Blackwell Companion to Zoroastrianism*. London: Wiley-Blackwell.

Swinburne, R. (1998). *Providence and the Problem of Evil*. Oxford: Clarendon Press.

Vasunia, P. (2007). The Philosophers' Zarathushtra. In C. Tuplin (ed.), *Persian Responses: Political and Cultural Interaction With(in) the Achaemenid Empire*. Swansea: Classical Press of Wales, pp. 237–266.

West, E. W. (trans.) (1882). *Pahlavi Texts Part II, Sacred Books of the East vol. 18*. Oxford: Oxford University Press. www.avesta.org/mp/dd.htm and https://sacred-texts.com/zor/sbe18/index.htm.

(1885). *Pahlavi Texts Part III, Sacred Books of the East vol. 24*. Oxford: Oxford University Press. The Menog i-Khrad, www.avesta.org/mp/mx.html and the whole of West's volume can be found at https://sacred-texts.com/zor/sbe24/index.htm.

Williams, A. V. (1983). *The Pahlavi Rivayat Accompanying the Dadestan i Denig*, PhD thesis, School of Oriental and African Studies, University of London.

Williams, B. (1970). The Self and the Future. *Philosophical Review*, 79(2), 161–180. https://doi.org/10.2307/2183946.

Williamson, T. (1994). *Vagueness*. New York: Routledge.

Acknowledgements

Thanks to Sara Bernstein, Laura Callahan, Mohsen Moghri, Michael Rea, Emily Thomas, and audiences at the Ultimate Reality/Divinity as the Ground: exploring the Structure of Reality Workshop at the University of Birmingham, and the Center for the Philosophy of Religion at the University of Notre Dame for helpful feedback and encouragement. Thanks also to an anonymous referee for saving me from some misunderstandings and for many suggestions for more discussion. Limitations of space prevented me from acting on many of these. Finally, thanks to Yujin Nagasawa for inviting me to contribute this Element and for encouragement along the way. Funding from the McMahon-Hank Professorship at the University of Notre Dame made it possible for this Element to be published open access, making the digital version freely available for anyone to read and reuse under a Creative Commons licence.

Cambridge Elements

Global Philosophy of Religion

Yujin Nagasawa
University of Oklahoma

Yujin Nagasawa is Kingfisher College Chair of the Philosophy of Religion and Ethics and Professor of Philosophy at the University of Oklahoma. He is the author of *The Problem of Evil for Atheists* (2024), *Maximal God: A New Defence of Perfect Being Theism* (2018), *Miracles: A Very Short Introduction* (2018), *The Existence of God: A Philosophical Introduction* (2011), and *God and Phenomenal Consciousness* (2008), along with numerous articles. He is the editor-in-chief of *Religious Studies* and served as the president of the British Society for the Philosophy of Religion from 2017 to 2019.

About the Series

This Cambridge Elements series provides concise and structured overviews of a wide range of religious beliefs and practices, with an emphasis on global, multi-faith viewpoints. Leading scholars from diverse cultural backgrounds and geographical regions explore topics and issues that have been overlooked by Western philosophy of religion.

Cambridge Elements

Global Philosophy of Religion

Elements in the Series

Afro-Brazilian Religions
José Eduardo Porcher

The African Mood Perspective on God and the Problem of Evil
Ada Agada

Contemporary Pagan Philosophy
Eric Steinhart

Semi-Secular Worldviews and the Belief in Something Beyond
Carl-Johan Palmqvist and Francis Jonbäck

Zoroastrianism and Contemporary Philosophy
Daniel Nolan

A full series listing is available at: www.cambridge.org/EGPR

Printed by Libri Plureos GmbH in Hamburg, Germany